GREGORY M. SCOTT

THE ASCENSION DICTATIONS

- GOD
- BEINGS OF Light
- ARCHANGELS
- LIGHT GIVERS
- ASCENDED MASTERS
  ○ LESSONS

BALBOA.PRESS

A DIVISION OF HAY HOUSE

Balboa Press books may be ordered through booksellers or by contacting:

Balboa Press
A Division of Hay House
1663 Liberty Drive
Bloomington, IN 47403
www.balboapress.com
844-682-1282

Because of the dynamic nature of the Internet, any web addresses or links contained in
this book may have changed since publication and may no longer be valid. The views
expressed in this work are solely those of the author and do not necessarily reflect the views
of the publisher, and the publisher hereby disclaims any responsibility for them.

The author of this book does not dispense medical advice or prescribe the use of any technique as a form
of treatment for physical, emotional, or medical problems without the advice of a physician, either directly
or indirectly. The intent of the author is only to offer information of a general nature to help you in your quest
for emotional and spiritual well-being. In the event you use any of the information in this book for yourself,
which is your constitutional right, the author and the publisher assume no responsibility for your actions.

Any people depicted in stock imagery provided by Getty Images are models,
and such images are being used for illustrative purposes only.
Certain stock imagery © Getty Images.

Scripture quotations marked KJV are from the Holy Bible, King James Version
(Authorized Version). First published in 1611. Quoted from the KJV Classic
Reference Bible, Copyright © 1983 by The Zondervan Corporation.

ISBN: 978-1-9822-5381-3 (sc)
ISBN: 978-1-9822-5382-0 (e)

Print information available on the last page.

Balboa Press rev. date: 10/23/2020

WELCOME TO THE ASCENSION DICTATIONS!

YES, IT'S ME. GOD. WHO ELSE BUT?
WHO ELSE COULD WELCOME YOU BUT ME?
CERTAINLY, NOT GREGORY M. SCOTT, EDD
Gregory is only *the transcriber just as you have a court reporter*
at trials, Gregory's job is to report what we say or said.

I should say welcome and congratulations because you are at the pinnacle of your spiritual achievement. No matter how many books, you have read, how many masters you have followed, how many spiritual paths upon which you have trod. This as far as you can go without my permission. In the meantime, there are a few things you should know. If you do not believe in Me, if you do not accept reincarnation as a fact, if you do not have a strong spiritual practice, you really need go no further with these dictations. And, most importantly, if you do not believe there are greater spiritual heights, so to speak, beyond those you have experienced, this work is not for you just yet. Maybe down the road, but not now. If you are already an energy worker, able to detect energy you're your palms, inner vision or scans, so much the better.

As you read this, you may notice slight tingling, energy surging through your body or your crown chakra expanding. Even your heart center might be opening just a bit. How you experience ME will differ widely, but be assured, what is here is for you alone Keep this to yourself.

In this moment, I am widening the connection between you and ME.

Bear in Mind, these are not conversations or chats along the lines of what I did in several volumes with Neale Donald Walsch. These are dictations, plain and simple: dictations by Me, Beings of Light, Archangels and Ascended Masters, You need to read these words carefully, then ignore them so that you will be completely open to the experience of ME, opinions without mental interference of thought, words and beliefs

What we all have written is solely to whet your appetite and activate your Ascension.

How does Ascension work? First you must ask for and get My permission to enter my Kingdom. If you get it, then, it's on.

If you don't get permission, not, It means something that you haven't let go is blocking you. Quite often, it's in the area of forgiveness, anger and/or some lower emotion letting go is what pros you into higher domains.

If I give you MY permission to Ascend, you must ask ME to eliminate any blockages between the heavenly kingdom and you. (You are asking, in fact, that your karma be eliminated.) I

If I grant your request, it will be immediately done.

You may notice a change in your state of consciousness and your perception of your spiritual reality. Most notice that something is different.

If not, Ascension may be something for which you are not ready at this time. Nevertheless, later on, you may notice a shift

At this moment you are in My Soul Domain, which is known by other names such as sartori, jivan mukti, the void, the Eckshar, all signifying a higher level of awareness, i.e. Soul Realization, however this state of consciousness is known in cultures across the world.

The truth of the matter is that for most, these are aspiration, seldom achieved for anyone but the spiritual master and the successor Were the followers to be admitted to this state, likely they would see no need to cling to the Master's coat taits in hope of higher experiences. Note that such masters leave their devotees to wallow in the shoals of karma, unable to dissolve their karmic loads. Even if the Master takes the devotee's karma, it's momentary and quite brief. He will not keep the karma for long. He only does it to tie the devotee more tightly to help the devotee know what it's like to be karma free These leaves devotee like a dog panting after the Master in hope of repeating the experience

Jesus offered the opportunity to be relieved of their heavy burden. I have given no other Master before with such power. The experience of Soul Realization is truly wonderful, to be sure. But it is only temporary because you will be buffeted even more so by the negative aspects of life determined to submerge you back into the word of cause and effects. Unfortunately, your success of being permanently karma free will not occur until you experience God Realization by moving further into my Kingdom, so to speak. Do not misunderstand me, all

Soul Realization experiences, even those I grant, are temporary. Unit I permit you to experience God Realization you will always be in the worlds o cause and effect. with God Realization, you are karma-free.

Let ME repeat this.

with God Ascension, you are karma-free.

This process for both Soul Ascension and God Ascension is well described at the following link (now in the world wide web archives.

Having said all this, let ME tell you how these works are organized. First, there is a dictation by my emissaries, "Beings of Light", that pushed and prodded Gregory nightly to publish these dictations.

They would not let Gregory sleep until he reached out to publishers. These dictations were originally intended for a relatively small group of energy workers. In the meantime, if you want a quick overview of the Ascension program as it was promulgated by the now disbanded Light Givers International Association, here's the link:

https://web.archive.org/web/20130922075253/http://lightgivers.org/index.htm

First, there is a dictation by My emissaries, Beings of Light. Next are My twelve sobering dictations. Next, comes dictations by Archangels' that chose anonymity, to help readers rely on the truth of what is written rather than their Archangelic credentials. Next is a series of lessons that were dictated by several Ascended masters. Lastly, in the main body of this document, there are never before revealed secret teachings by several Ascended Masters to help Gregory toward spiritual mastership that he stoutly refused. (He didn't refuse the teachings, but he declined the master robe).

Transcriber, Yes! Spiritual Master or Messenger. No!

Finally, there is an Appendix chock full of bits and pieces. These include slightly edited versions of Chapters One, Two and Three of the transcribed book, The Universal Healer; God Energy in Action to help explain how Gregory became My transcriber. There are copies of newsletters written over the years, his healer and professional resumes, presumably to indicate that he had a professional career, in addition to his night time duties for Me. There are a few sexy biographic descriptions and testimonials that might be of interest, along with a course proposal that was never implemented. If you get that far, or if you read ahead, he includes a self-test that energy workers might use in some way. I will let you figure that out. Again, welcome to the heavenly gates. I bid you enter albeit temporary. free of karma, so the experience of Soul Realization, also known as sartori, jivan mukti, the void can be yours – permanently. Again, welcome the pinnacle of your spiritual journey. From here there is no journey

Be yourself Ascended to ME,

CONTENTS

A MESSAGE FROM GREGORY

You are about to read material that I never expected to be made public. These are personal dictations that I received for individuals in training to be Ascension Masters. However, in March 2020, I was awakened and told to make these materials available to the general public. For those unfamiliar with dictations as I originally, dictations are somewhat similar to the "still small voice" mentioned often in religious materials. However, they are not still and they are not small. They are amplified and clearly heard inside your head and not by your ears. The dictaters said they could be referred to as, "Beings of Light," and distinguished themselves from the Universal Healers, the Ascended Masters, the Light Givers/Ascension Masters. The second section of this introduction presents verbatim the dictations that I transcribed. I recorded. At this time, I do not know what will happen after this book is published. I am retired both from my careers. I was a priest in one organization and a master in another[1], both relatively obscure guru-centered spiritual teachings. In the former, I was a widely sought speaker and workshop facilitator and for the latter, with an advanced spiritual master, I was introduced to the experience of dictations by telling ME that I was going to write a book, the dialogue went like this:

Owens: You are going to write a book.

Scott: Oh Yeah, the last book I wrote was my doctoral dissertation, I'm not going to write another.

Owens: Yes, you are. It will be called the "The Universal Healer."

Scott: "I don't know anything about that. How am I going to write a book about something I don't.

Owens: You aren't going to write it, it will be dictated to you.

Scott: Dictation, how does that work?

Owens: I'll give you a set of questions. once you type each question, you will hear the answer.

Scott: Are you serious?

---

[1] Gregory was co-founder and served as president, 2004-2005

As a native skeptic, born in Missouri, the "Show Me" state, I had to see if worked. To my utter amazement, it worked and resulted, by 2006 in a 158 page book, "the Universal Healer," that, at this writing is not yet available for publication. After I finished it, I conducted a few small Universal Healer workshops during 2005-2009. Things remained quiet for a year or so, then the dictations started up again. For the book, the individuals dictating identified themselves by name and capacity, I.e., Archangel this or that or Ascended Master, this or that. Except for thef Ascended Master dictations, these new dictations were generated anonymously. They said they wanted readers to appreciate their dictations for the truth contained therein, not by the title of the alleged dictater. So, each was signed as "The Light Givers." Along the way, we created a "Light Giver" The webpage offers the direct experience of Soul Ascension and explained God Ascension

In all honesty, I will admit to having received a couple boosts that made ME more receptive to the dictations.

The first came after a from my spiritual teacher in which he told that Archangel Michael had a ceremony for me. To experience it, I need to go into contemplation, which I did. Instantly, wide awake, inwardly, I found myself on my knees before a group of Archangels. The Archangel held his hands apart, a ball of light materialized that immediately was transferred into my heart center.

A few weeks later, again, inwardly, I received a series of initiations in the company of many spiritual masters in to whose membership I was admitted as an a plunged into a column of light.

It was a wonderful and amazing experience, far beyond my wildest imaginings. **Universal Healer** was transcribed shortly thereafter.

By 2011, The Universal Healer program had morphed into the Light Giver International Association and three complete sets of dictations by the Light Givers along with a website and facebook page.

The last in the series, but the first here is the, "God Messages." was transcribed after a Pentacostal Prophet came up to the pew where I was sitting.

She said, and said the following to me, "I have a message for you from God."

"No more intermediaries, you speak with ME directly"

Although I had this gift of being able to get dictations from practically any being in the higher worlds, even Jesus, I wanted, despite Neal Donald Walsch's wonderful exchanges with God, I lacked both the curiosity and the temerity to initiate such conversations on my own, So I did.

S/He talked. I transcribed. All in All, I received 12 God dictations. They came almost as fast as I could record them.

What is Ascension?

Ascension provides is quite simply the experience of being in the Kingdom of Heaven while still in the physical body. What the Beings of Light are wont to do, as was the original Light Giver program, is to equip and embed quickly the spiritually qualified with the direct experience so that they do so with others. By "spiritually qualified," it means those that are at the pinnacle of their religious or spiritual path and that that no preacher, pastor, prophet or spiritual leader can perform the connection with God that will result in your permanent Ascension in the Kingdom of Heaven.

Are You Ready? Read on. Next, the Beings of Light, Then the surprising God dictations.

WHO ARE WE? BEINGS OF LIGHT

Quite simply we are direct expressions of the force that is the creative intelligence that brought all galaxies, universes and solar systems into being and by extension, all sentient life, including human beings, as well. You humans have a passion for definition and distinctions. What or who are beings of Light? 'what are Beings of Light? Who connotes an gender identity and a personality that is distinct from other individual gender personalities.

What is the reference in that our distinction is related to our association, so to speak with the 'creative intelligence no doubt you are familiar with the concepts of angels, archangels, gods, devils, karma, goodness, spiritual, sin and the like. We use the term concept loosely because they "but Divine ideas established to permit sentient beings in your world against which to shape and understand the nature of what might be called 'Divine reality and come to be established completely within the quadrant of Divine essence of their universe, these are all distinct from the term, "infinity," which, from now on, we will use to refer to the Creative Intelligence that spawned these idea through subordinate levels of reality. Let us be clear, infinity lies outside above or beyond these concepts. Truly it may not be characterized, depicted or described. One might be tempted to say, "It just IS." But even that is limiting in that, the alternative is that, it could be, "Is Not." There is no alternative to infinity. Again, it has no assignable character. All the others are assumed or assigned particular characteristics, in which they are cast. There is a disturbance in the Force. That is that each quadrant of every solar system, universe and galaxy maintains a distribution of creative essence that rotates and renews on its own, sentient beings regularly in cyclic order. Your quadrant has experienced a substantial delay. We are here to accelerate the process. That will be done by "helping" those that are stymied in their efforts to return or "Ascend" "to Source." Note the use of "Ascend" and "Source." Source denutes the aspect of the Creative Intelligence active within a particular quadrant. Ascend denotes the integration of the intelligence and beingness of sentient beings within the aspect of Source within which they live and breathe. Understand this. Source is not a unitary phenomenon. Aspects of each occur and interact within sentient beings within their own quadrant of Creative Inrelligence. We need thousands, if not millions of individuals in your world that seek Ascension to make themselves known to us.

Already there are several individuals that we identify as "'Ascension Helpers" trained and aligned to act as catalysts in the Ascension process. The lead human, at thi time, for this process is "Gregory Michael Scott, EdD, the recorder of this message. Dr. Scott worked for years with our counterparts in the Archangelic community to establish an activity similar to what we propose. First, there was the Universal Healer, focused mainly on expanding individuals healing capabilities and experiences. He conducted several small workshops in various U.S. cities. This morphed into the Light Givers, with a not too dissimilar process, offer too Ascension that offered no workshops of any consequence. Yet this morphed into Light Givers/Ascension Masters for which there were no workshops or clients. The entire sequence ended in 2017, 'through the entire process it occurred neither to Dr. Scott nor the 'archangelic community to make his work available via world wide publication.

Let us be clear, what distinguished the process above from all other teaching-learning process on your planet on your planet, is that it is an energetic process-replication process. 'Specifically, those individuals that Source accepted as spiritually qualified were clarified to three levels of spiritual beingness. By being spiritually qualified, these individuals had reached the pinnacles of their spiritual path and have seen through the facilities of spiritual hierarchies and the limitations of healing and spiritual hierarchies. They yearn for higher realities and know that the path they have travelled can yield no further results. There are no workshops, classes or spiritual masters empowered to lead them ahead. In fact, there has only been one who could say, "I am the Way." That being, Jesus Christ, is no longer in human embodiment and those that would speak in his name are most often poor examples of his teaching. In fact, many have used his name to enrich themselves with money, cars and houses. They adorn themselves with spiritually vacant titles and truly distract their followers from the true purpose of Jesus's earthly teaching, simply that one could safely become integrated with the Divine Essenced, which they know as God. Indeed, Jesus prayer at Gethsemane is powertfully illustrative of that conviction.

This aside, the process allows those that are so endowed to support the endowment of others with the capacity to dialogue directly with Source and, if permitted, to eliminate the many distractions that hinder such integration. For the record, the support that is provided is both energetic and caltalytic. The Ascension helper's endowment stabilizes the connection and helps guide the candidates release of energetic distractions and limitations, such as sin, karma, guilt and so on. In succeeding dictations, we will discuss a number of related topics, the thrust of which are significantly different from the titillation of Neal Donald Walsch. While we notice that Walsch's materials are presentations of dialogues or conversations with God that are framed in a conversational mode. The information that we are sharing with your readers are dictations. While Walsch's materials have an elevating effect, that are not intended to be transformative. Ours are neither titillating, entertaining nor merely interesting. They are intended to be transformative and lay the groundwork for Ascension.[2]

Beings of Light

---

[2] this dictation was transcribed Mar. 4, 22020

THE POWER OF HEALING

Much has been made is being made by various healers, preachers and prophets of the healings that occur and are often associated with their work. What many do not understand is the true purpose of healing. And that is just one purpose, that being, to bring individuals closer to, if not, into the range of God. God, itself, myself, is known by many names, each of which is only a stopping point or way station to the true experience of Divinity.

Unfortunately, because of the allure and power of the human ego, both of the "spiritual teacher" and of the "seeker," arrival at the destination in the Kingdom of God is not only delayed in some cases, but thwarted in others. Why, in heaven's name are these preachers, teachers, and so called spiritual leaders and masters, convinced that their understanding of what I have said through others in the many holy books, is what they can understand.

The truth of the matter is that each word that I have uttered and has been repeated by my emissaries is embedded with my spiritual essence and is directed to upliftment and awareness of each individual at the Soul level. It would be far more elevating and real, if the pastor, preacher, or spiritual teacher simply presented my words to the congregation and asked them, now, "What is God saying to us here," instead of trying to narrow it to his or her understanding, which, you must believe, is always much less than what I had in mind.

In this message, I want to help you understand the true purpose of healing. Believe me, it is not to make life better. It is not to improve relationships. It is not to improve your finances. It is not to help you find a job. And, it is most certainly not to increase your reliance on your pastor, preacher or prophet for guidance in your life. The purpose of healing today, as it was in Jesus' time, is to demonstrate that the Kingdom of God is truly at hand which, in this case, means that Ascension to a higher state of being is truly available.

Can you see just how simple this is? Jesus offered a shortcut. He told people that if they will accept him in his responsibility which I will say was as the ultimate transformer and vehicle to the Divine experience, then it can be received. Of course, the Divine experience needs be preceded by the removal of all negativities, called by some, karma, and in the Christian context, sin. So much is made in the Bible of being cleansed and made white as snow, the point being that Ascension requires the relinquishing of karma/sin.

Understand this, you can live a life that is oriented toward your past deeds and transgressions. And, you can live a life that celebrates your past accomplishments that looks forward to even more. Both of these approaches fail to achieve, in any regard, what I require of you in the human condition. You must live your life focused on the immediacy of the Kingdom of Heaven or to recast that, of the availability of the Ascended state of consciousness.

Understand this. And, this is something that you have heard many times before, but not from ME directly. Your life as a human being is simply an illusion that I have given you. There is but one purpose: to solidify your very Beingness in the Kingdom of God. Your choices are quite simple. Are you solidly in the world and traps of illusion, overcome by the very illusory nature of the human condition? Or are you solidly in the Kingdom of God, in the Ascended state? When Jesus said the Kingdom of Heaven is within, he was not pointing to a future time or event. He was and is identifying immediate possibilities. So, healing that occurs without reference to the ultimate state of Being or without reference to the Divine Being itself is such a meaningless gesture, much as pouring cups of sea water back into the ocean has no effect on the depth, composition or tides of the ocean.

Some might say, well, it was probably easier for people in Jesus' time to accept that the Kingdom of God was at hand because he worked many miracles that included raising the dead, casting out demons and healing people by the thousands. That might be so, but consider this. The leaders had no regard for him or his work and worked mightily to eliminate him. Moreover, the disciples may never have really gotten his message or truly understood Him. He stayed around for days teaching them and working with them to help them understand what he wanted them to do.

Observe that the one individual responsible for the propagation of Christianity, Saint Paul, was not among the group of disciples that travelled with Jesus. Indeed, he never met Jesus physically. Yet his profound insights shape most of the writings in the New Testament that follow the accounts of those who were with Jesus and who captured some of his sayings.

Likewise, you can access the same font of wisdom that Paul drew upon by focusing, not upon your healing experiences, but rather upon what they portend, in terms of greater access to not only your personal Divinity but the very essence of Divinity itself.

Be Yourself Ascended.

GOD MESSAGE #2

WHY SIN EXISTS, MORE OR LESS

Today I will explain to you the concept of sin that has evolved for two reasons: the need humans have to regret and my need for correction of the human viewpoint. Sin plainly and simply persists because of the guilt that humankind desires as the result of actions taken. The truth of the matter is that humans refuse to have what could be called a "more or less" consciousness. That is a viewpoint that lives in the middle ground and which seeks no absolutes.

Let ME be clear here. The essential problem with humans is that they seek to live in the world of absolutes. And in so doing, they are confined to one corner of life or the other. The "more or less" consciousness, if it were in a room, would be squarely in the middle of the room, if at all. Most likely, it would be floating somewhere above the room and not looking down or up. It would just be. Sin is linked with its cousin judgment that finds fault with the actions not only of others, but also of oneself.

In the "more or less "consciousness, sin does not exist. Why? Because it does not harbor action residue from past actions. In fact, it is completely disconnected from its past actions. It does not disavow the results of its past actions. But it neither dwells nor focuses its attention on the past. This is a hard concept for most to grasp. It's much like a swimmer floating the ocean that notices the waves buffeting his body. Does it make sense for him to count the waves, measure their height, calculate their mass, even the seconds between the waves? Of course not. Then why focus on the sea of events that occur in one's life?

Now, I am not saying that you humans should not take notice of what occurs in your lives. And, I am not saying that you should not understand the consequences of actions that you have taken. The operational term is "dwell." You should not dwell upon them to the extent that most of you do. Understand that you have a tendency not just to dwell upon your actions, but to dwell within them. To the extent, that if actions taken by you were a bubble, you live within the bubble rather than above it. I am spending this time elaborating on this tendency because it is truly the greatest cause and explanation for the existence of sin.

Understand that using the "more or less" approach is to elevate the consciousness above the human tendency to seek absolutes and the tendency to reduce units of awareness into finite elements. Of course, units of awareness can be seen as finite elements. But the truth of the matter is that consciousness is that which is doing the seeing of the finite elements. Do you get the point? Either you see yourself as being within the finite elements, which is something that many people do, such as, "You're late!" "No, I'm not." "Well, actually, I'm just two minutes late." In each case, the individual has defined time as if it were encapsulating.

See how freeing it would be for the person to say, "I am neither late nor on time; I am here in this moment." Can you sense that the freedom in this last statement could be restated as, "Actually, I am really on time, more or less." Take that another step and say in reply, "You dwell in time but I dwell in God," which is really what matters. Of course, knowing that your friend dwells in time, you could consider it an act of love to be on time, more or less. Sin, to restate the point, is clearly the result of mankind's practice of dwelling within.

So, what is being dwelt within? What is being dwelt within is the sum and substance of regrets, feelings of lack, of more than abundance, of insufficiency, or sufficiency, of wrongful deeds received and committed and so on. It is a collective blanket in which you humans have immersed yourselves and from which only Divine forgiveness may allow you to escape. Regret of the past is the harbinger of future regrets. Even if one vows to make the same mistake never again, the mere fact of having made the vow, much as muddy shoes track a white rug, so does the vow carry into one's future the mud from the past. This then sharpens the distinction made elsewhere by the Lightgivers between absolution and forgiveness. While forgiveness preserves for all time the memory of a transgression, absolution wipes the slate clean as if it has never happened. Another human can forgive, but only I, God, either directly or through one of my emissaries, can absolve your sin.

This does not mean that you have lost the power to sin. But even that can be taken away from you, to the extent that the sinning thought or action may not reoccur. While Catholic priests believe that the power of absolution has been granted to them, there is, to put it plainly, a lie under which they operate. So, it is pure fiction when they say to one of their charges that their sins have been forgiven. What is a lie is that the priests think, in their own minds, that they are operating with the power of absolution. It is not a lie that their sins are forgiven because that is what my Son Jesus did a long time ago. If they have accepted him as their savior then their sins are forgiven.

What is forgotten is that whenever Jesus said, "Thy sins are forgiven," he would add, "Go Thy way and sin no more." What is not known by many is that with the last statement, he removed from the recipient the capacity to sin again. In modern times, if he were a smoker, he would throw his pack of cigarettes away. If he were a drinker, he would empty his whisky bottles. If he were a porn addict, he would not log on to porn sites.

Note the use earlier of emissaries instead of messengers. Messengers merely preach my word. Often times they are masters, sometimes vested with amazing powers and abilities. These come in the form of masters, spiritual teachers, and so on. Their responsibility is to point the way to ME and to step out of the way so that you might engage with me. My emissaries emerge from my heart. They fully reside in ME and I reside in them. They have come directly from my heart, as did Jesus. I have allowed you to witness Jesus' birth as a ball of light coming directly from my spiritual essence. Or, their emergence from my heart occurred after a very long and arduous journey through human incarnations that culminated in a re-entry into and re-emergence from my heart.

The training that the emissaries receive during their journey is one related to their need to be able to communicate with humankind and to perform what seem to be miracles in my name. Whatever limitations they have in regard to manifesting my glory or making my glory manifest is related to either their self-imposed limitations or limits that I have placed upon them, based on the life track that I have set them upon. Although, in the eyes of others, they may have committed some sinful actions, in my eyes they and all humans, are without sin, Most importantly, in their own eyes, they are without sin because I have removed the concept of sin from their consciousness and their being.

Thus, they transcend their entire history that spans time and space, infinite worlds, indeed infinity itself, and are sin free. In fact, each of these is but a unit of awareness that, in all truth, my emissaries are outside of. The glue that holds humankind to sin is the power of regret. My emissaries have no regret. How could they? Better yet, why should they? They know that all losses are counterbalanced by equivalent gains. And that all joy is counterbalanced by pain. All sorrow is counterbalanced by gladness. Everything is more or less, which is the way it should be. More or less, with no regrets.

Sin, as it is, is a phenomenon localized to the worlds of causality. Contrary to popular beliefs, sin has nothing to do with the perfecting of Soul. Soul as it is represents ME and is fully endowed with my spiritual essence is already perfect. What is, indeed, perfected, as it were, is the individual's viewpoint. That being, what is required is the ability to function in all states of existence with a viewpoint that is centered upon me. To say "upon" misstates what is required, which is a viewpoint that is not only within, but at my core. In such case, my thoughts are yours. My voice is yours. My spiritual essence operates your entire body. You have no dreams, except of me. You have no hunger except for me. You seek no light except of me. In the Bible, this is spoken of as the Holy Ghost, which is my active intelligence in your worlds.

Have no regrets. Say to yourself daily on a moment by moment basis, "Thank God, I have no regrets." With the reading of this, the energy of regret is removed and you are completely freed of Sin or any tendency to Sin, if that is your request. More than being forgiven, you are now absolved. Absolution is an action of ME or one of my emissaries. However, I cannot or will not remove your tendency to regret. That occurs as a function of free will.

Regret is a human tendency. So, humans need to drop the tendency to mentally harbor regrets. It may be even easier to inventory those things for which you feel regret and to say for each, "I have no regrets," Or, simply say to yourself, "Of all the things that I have done in life I have no regrets." To take it a bit farther, rather than saying, "I wish I had done" something different, instead you might say, "If **I had** done something different, it might have turned out differently more or less, but I have no regrets." More or Less.

LOVE

To say "I love you" understates the reality of this love. The short form of this reality is that I am you. The ultimate form of this love was expressed by Jesus when, in his prayer to ME he said, "I am in you, Father, and you are in me". In other words, the ultimate form of love is experienced in true undifferentiated oneness. Jesus spent as much time in prayer as he did because it is necessary to keep a sustained attention on this oneness. What makes the act of loving one another is the fact that, as humans, by definition, you appear to be separate from each other and are, in fact, differentiated. Although there are many expressions of me, such as you are, I am truly undifferentiated.

There are some necessary obstacles to your achieving this level of undifferentiation with each other or even with me. For most, such obstacles seem somewhat insurmountable. Yet I see all of them as simple petty minor differences originated by what has happened to you before you realized your need for me. The whole purpose of your petty existence is to help you realize that the so-called insurmountable is generally and genuinely insignificant. Frankly, I am underwhelmed by all that you experience as overwhelming. Understand this, no matter how much you long for ME and want to be in my hear; no matter how fervent your prayers, your petitions, your screams of devotion; no matter how great your sacrifices, how long your fasts, how intense your pieties, you will not enter my heart until you have freedom yourself of your self-imposed bondage.

But, it's not your fault you insist. Your mother was this and that. Your father was this and that. Your brother was this and that. You were raped, beaten and abused at a very early age. Life was hard and on and on. If you entered a room and saw a rope on the floor and a rafter above your head with a ladder standing just below the rafter, you might trip over the rope, bump into the ladder, but does that mean you might automatically hang yourself? In the afterlife, would you say to some that you felt obliged to hang yourself because all that was there? Of course not. You might say instead, all that was there, but I chose not to hang myself and decided to jump rope and use the ladder to paint the ceiling and the rafter.

I have given you this obstacle-filled life. Why do you choose to hang yourself? Because of what you have experienced? Beloved, these obstacles not only diminish your capacity to experience me, in many cases, they block you from ME only because you permit them to. Only in rare cases do I step in, or the angels at my direction, to redirect a spiritual evolutionary path going awry from its pre-ordained trajectory for this incarnation. For this reason, years ago, Gregory was stuck in an downward atheistic trend. He met with others every Sunday morning at 11 am to discuss their disbelief in me. When he was pondering why such meetings were important to him I cleared many years of karma from his mind so he could think clearly and realize himself spiritually. It still took many years for him to begin directly communicating with me.

You each have infinite existence, yet you live finitely. By this, I mean, you have many fears: of the dark, the cold, of death and so on. The fear of death, quite frankly undergirds most fears. The greatest fear, often unarticulated, is the fear of being finite, i.e. of passing into non-existence. This is ridiculous. Death is but a doorway. One that you step through and you live continuously. With each lifetime, you learn to expand your capacity to love and to overcome your fears even more, which brings you closer to my heart. This you do unaware until you come to the point where you are today, to read and hopefully understand these God dialogues personally given by the source of all wisdom, love, power and understanding.

How awesome is that? Just think, you are hearing directly from the Almighty about his love for you and ways in which to exist in your love for Him and His love for you. This may seem awfully abstract and far from the reality in which you live. Oh, no. This discussion hones directly into your own reality with the pinpoint accuracy of a laser beam. Consider this. If the whole purpose of your existence is more than to love ME or to experience my love for you, then the so-called obstacles in your love should be seen as love opportunities. Understand this, if you are incapable of living in a continuous loving state, then you have no hope of being continuously in my awareness and will be belched from my kingdom.

It is not enough that you have achieved my Holy presence. It is not enough that you perform meditations, exorcisms and cleansings. It is not enough that you have achieved high spiritual rank: pastor, bishop, apostle or even Pope. What matters is that you are continuously in my presence and that I am continuously in yours. This you can only do through continuous practice. How does that occur: by loving and blessing and thanking all that presents itself to you. I will give you all the support that I can through the spiritual teachers, angels and others that I send to you. But, at this stage of your existence, I cannot and will not override your freedom of choice.

You must always be intensely aware of what you must give up in order to be in my presence. Instead of focusing on what's been given up, focus on Me. It is not enough for ME to say that I am God; more so, it is important for you to say and understand that you are God, a fully developed expression of Me. Dwell on that thought. Now, can you see how the very idea of love blinks invitingly from my heart to yours? Love begins as a tiny strand and grows into a mighty link that ties you to my heart. In this moment, so that you can fully understand and get the import of this message, the view that separates you from living and acting in ME is lifted.

Can you see now the pattern of your life: the daily opportunities to express and Be in Love that you have foregone? Can you understand how separate you are from me? You need to live in my footprint instead of the one that you are currently standing in. Note with the veil lifted, the infusion of love that now abides. Hold that awareness; allow it to wash over you as Jesus did just before the soldiers took him. By no means am I suggesting that your focus be on loving others. Let your focus be on me. See others as my expressions seeded in your life solely so that you can love ME more.

PRAYER AND PETITION

Of all the connections and possible connections that I might have with humans, the most pitiful are prayers or petitions. The universes that I own, manage, and create are practically littered with the prayers of those that have the greatest opportunity for manifestation. I have vested each of you with the capacity to fully reflect, channel and transmit ME in MY fullness into every universe that you occupy. Your connections with ME are clogged with prayer. Yet you put before ME on a moment by moment basis your petty and pitiful concerns about needs in your transitory and ephemeral universe. Don't you get it? You are situated in the most temporary existence, one that fades and disappears from your view every 50 - 90 years or so. Why put so much attention on living a pain free, happy, pleasant life, when what only matters is eternal life.

Do you get it? Do you hear me? What only matters is eternal life. Some of you actually go to car dealerships or watch television commercials, pick out the car you want, and rather than going back home, to college, to trade school, wherever you can go to learn what you need to increase your earning power, you go home and ask ME in your prayers to give you the car. For a few of you this may work. Not because MY angels grant your wish, but because MY employee, known by you the negative power, in charge of the illusion, knows how exactly to hold you in that illusion: Grant your prayers.

Believe me, your so-called success with prayer is nothing but a tool to keep you even more tightly in the illusion in which you live. This may sound like some sort of deception. But the fact of the matter is, that if you cannot learn how to live outside the illusion, you will not be able to live in Me. I am spoken of as God, the eternal One, heaven, the Void and by many other names. Your world is constructed in such a way to help you develop the internal power to resist it. Once Gregory's Ex told him, "I can't believe that this is what this is all about!" Well, believe it or not, that's all I want of you. In fact, the word "resist" is too strong. Perhaps "ignore" might be even too strong. The greatest description is to "Be in the world, but not of it." I know most of you have heard that before, but do you get a sense of the non-action that I am speaking of here. To say you are actionless is even too strong. There is just nothing.

An old Negro spiritual has lyrics that say "Just like a tree standing by the water, I shall not be moved." And so it is. Your efforts at prayer, often thought to connect you to

Me, in fact, separate you even farther from me. Think about it. A prayer is like a push. It is not a climb up the ladder to God. It is a further descent down the spiritual ladder. When you pray, you are acknowledging even more so our separateness. I am over here, you are saying, and "God, you great dispenser of dates, husbands, wives, sex, cars and other things, dispense what I need so that MY worthless life may increase in value." Every time you think a prayer has been granted, you shout, sing and announce that God has granted your prayers. Such is not the case. I do not answer prayers. MY employees, whose job is to keep you even more firmly locked in those worlds, has answered your prayers.

Every answered prayer is nothing but a way to keep you from graduating into My heart. There is no rush for you to enter MY world. The only souls that need be here are those that have earned their way by discerning the truth and have abandoned their pitiful attempts to access me. Let ME speak plainly. I do not hear prayers. I cannot hear prayers. MY angels grant two types of prayers, those that are made by individuals chosen, like Jesus, to be my emissaries. And, you may have noticed that Jesus spent much of his time away from the crowds in prayer. The second type of prayers granted by my angels are for those that, by their devotion, have earned the right and for miracles that strengthen belief in Me. These show up quite often as the miracles performed by faith healers. Unfortunately, belief in ME is often not the result; it becomes more a case of belief in the healer.

I ask that you not petition, beg, demand or grovel. Worship and meditation are stronger tools, Not the most advanced, but stronger and more direct. I have vested within you the power to create and recreate the worlds around you. You have the choice to continue begging for crusts of bread when you are the baker; you own the flour, the ingredients, in fact, the kitchen and ovens themselves. Spend your time learning to live within Me, living through Me, manifesting Me. Meditation offers a greater opportunity to reach me, but even that has some limitations that I will point out in another dictation. Before I stop, a very few of you believe your prayers have been answered. In fact, you yourselves manifested your intention, which is what Jesus had in mind when He said, "Ask and it will be given to you; seek and you will find; knock and the door will be opened to you." This truly works when you and I are One. There is much more to be said, but I end this here.

GOD MESSAGE #5

MANIFESTATION

In MY most recent dictation, I rebuked your pitiful and selfish prayers that clog the lines between Thee and Me. In this dictation, I remind you of the power of manifestation that has been given you. This power is not unlike the power used to bring the worlds into manifestation. Recall, I said, "Let there be light," and there Is. So, this power is vested within you, too. Albeit buried beneath feelings of guilt, anger, loss, emotion, lack, memories of this life and others, the power of manifestation is within you. You each accept that Soul is a spark of God. Yet you ignore and envy what this means. This means not that you are given MY power, but you are MY power unmanifested.

So, what must you do to realize directly and completely this power. Must you strip off, painfully and deliberately, each aspect of yourself that obscures your true nature in hours and hours of psychiatric sessions? Does this mean that you must examine your parents' actions and inactions in order to invalidate their hold upon you? Does this mean that you must journal all your thoughts and feelings so that you can know the real you? No! What you must do is accept that each of those things is present and train yourself, yes, train yourself to rise above them, freeing yourself of their hold upon you. This being done, you begin to enter the worlds of true manifestation, MY world.

Now, how may this training may be done? While it is not painful, it is deliberate. Remember, you are what you put your attention upon. Indeed, the more your attention is upon it, the more you become it. Does this sound farfetched to you? Think of the people you have known that were "into" something like cars, clothes or even sex. To a great extent these people were what their attention was upon. The quote, "As a man thinketh, so is he," points this out. Thinking is more of a mental process. In this case, it's less thinking; it's Being. Lyrics in a country and western song years ago said, "Your lips may be near, but where is your heart?" By the same token, if you wish to manifest the essence of me, your attention must be on Me. This does not mean that you should not pray for MY help in this regard. That prayer I will answer to help you move to a higher form of connection with me.

The higher forms include worship, gratitude, Oneness and Manifestation. While it may be possible for someone to move from the selfish prayer directly to manifestation, it is unlikely. What needs to occur is a fundamental reorientation of one's beingness that can only occur through systematic spiritual application that goes far beyond the brief prayer in the morning, a few words over meals and a quick prayer while falling asleep. What you must do is steep yourself in the Holy Ghost. You must ask ME to fill you with the Holy Ghost and that it lift you and sustain your presence in MY kingdom. You must spend as much of your time during the day allowing your random thoughts to be of Me. Recognize that everything that comes to you, good and bad, is a gift from ME to you that allows you to be grateful. Can you see how you are retraining yourself to be manifestor of love?

Understand this; you cannot be in MY kingdom if you are unable to sustain yourself in love. This does not mean that you will not have moments, but it does mean that your natural state of being must become Divine. It is not enough to recognize once or twice a day, that your true nature is Divine in origin. You must begin even more so to deepen your beingness in me. This is not the first time you have heard this. But it is the first time you have heard it from me. You must make ME the center point of your life and breathe MY spiritual essence with every breath you take. Does this make you a God fanatic? No. What it does is make good use of the time you spend worrying, plotting, planning, spacing out, being emotionally upset, watching television, fussing fighting and so on.

To make this point, take any one day and keep a journal of how you spend your time. Remember that what you put your attention on is what you become. Your journal will reveal to you how littered your life is with things that are completely non-essential. The goal of complete manifestation is to be so completely absorbed in ME and I in you that your needs are met effortlessly, and do not need long prayers or extended begging. If the spiritual need is there I will fill it.

Understand that your needs fulfilled are those that make you a greater instrument. MY needs are consistent with yours that support the eternal consciousness, as some say "Kingdom Work." So, the preachers, pastors and prophets that accumulate great wealth, allegedly in MY name, are an abomination to ME and have no place in MY Kingdom. They foul the air with their greediness and I will spit them out of MY mouth into the depths of Hell.

GRATITUDE

Of the many "virtues" spoken of, probably the least understood and practiced is gratitude. By gratitude, I do not mean simpy the art of saying "Thank You." The gratitude of which I speak is far greater, more extensive and more powerful than that. It is, in fact, a state of being, a way of life. It is the art of livingness. I will say this quite simply, the individual that is incapable of living completely and fully in a state of gratitude will be unable to sustain existence in MY kingdom.

This is a state that must be cultivated deliberately. It is akin to a state of being aware of blessing and quite related. In order to cultivate gratitude, one must go to sleep at night being aware of all the good and happy things that have occurred during the day and awake with a similar expectation. All other things that have occurred during the day should also be acknowledged with a feeling of joy and happiness that they have occurred. Elsewhere I have indicated that you must keep your attention on ME during the day. Now, I suggest that you expand that attention to include an awareness of gratitude. It is not enough for you to be grateful to ME for your existence. It is necessary for you to be grateful to yourself for your existence.

Understand this. The fact that you are aware of your existence is less testimony to me, but more testimony to yourself. The problem is that you really don't know what to do with your existence. Your attention flits like a moth from point to point, issue to issue, emotion to emotion. Be steadfast with your attention. Fix your attention upon ME and your inner awareness upon gratitude. Practice expanding your awareness, but keep it clear of intrusions.

Think of nothing else but ME and your gratitude for the existence of which you are aware. If you choose bring into your awareness all of the things and persons for which you are grateful. Hold the feeling. Then, let them fade out of your awareness. Hold the feeling. Allow your attention to shift to the many things for which you have little or no gratitude. Now, allow the feeling of gratitude to wash over them. These could be things like your neighbors, their homes, their children, school buildings, classrooms. Do you get the point?

There is nothing of which you are aware for which you should not feel grateful. Your own awareness is the mechanism from which gratitude truly must spring. It is not enough for you to prostrate yourself before the Almighty professing your undying love and gratitude. It is not enough that you populate your consciousness with the things and persons that bring you joy or not. It is not enough, even for you to notice the people and things with which you might spread and share your gratitude. Why?

Because your gratitude must flow outward and inward, unbroken by any feelings of separation, much as the ocean tides roll, flow and crash upon the shore, all unbroken and continuous. But, most importantly, you have to understand that if there are any discontinuities in your gratitude, they are flaws in your spiritual beingness, thereby ejecting you from MY eternal consciousness.

Yes, love, devotion, and worship are all important. But of these, gratitude is given the least attention. It is the Divine glue that holds MY universes together. The sun, moon and the stars themselves would spin out of their orbits were it not for gratitude. It is greater than gravity. It is more powerful that the centripetal and centrifugal forces. In the higher worlds, it is known by another name and is at the core of creation, the infinite cause of all that Is. But in your world, you know it as gratitude, which is but a hint of the infinite majesty and possibility that gratitude anticipates.

Maintain, expand and enjoy extended gratitude. Some say, "Be grateful." Instead, I say, "Be gratitude." Make that your way of life, your way of Being. Unless you are in that state, you will not enter MY Kingdom.

Spend the time you have in this existence learning how to bathe, luxuriate and immerse yourself in gratitude. Life, indeed, the very meaning of life will take on a meaning that you did not know was possible.

GOD MESSAGE #7

REALIZATION AND SUPPOSITION

In a Light Giver Message, much is made of the distinction of the spiritual mind. In this dictation, I will sharpen that distinction even more by highlighting the importance of realization. Most of your readers probably would like to learn how to transcend the spiritual mind. The problem is that learning is not involved. It is not a mental activity. One can no more learn how to transcend the mind than a basketball could propel itself though a hoop.

To be sure, I have instilled within the human being the power of imagination. That power is akin to MY power of creation, the capacity to summon within one's thought forms the shape and texture of something that is to be physically manifested or brought into being. Note that I say it is "akin" to the power of creation. What escapes most that use the power of imagination is that there is an underlying and temporary transformation of their internal reality. It is not the imagining that causes manifesting, it is the temporary shift in their internal reality. When I, the Divine I, exercise the power of creation, there is no thought involved, what comes into being is perfect in that moment. The shape and form of it emerges from MY Being. There is no explanation or understanding of it, it just Is.

When the human being exercises the power of imagination, it occurs, nevertheless, within his reality frame, and is a human realization. What he has learned and is demonstrating is how to transcend the limitations of his reality frame, but the shift is impermanent. Why? It is because he reverts back to the reality frame in which he is situated, once the manifestation exercise has completed.

Consider the difference between supposition and realization. Supposition requires the individual to mock up or to imagine a state or situation different from what is. Supposition only exists in the mental framework of the supposer. Realization, by contrast is a recognition of what exists within the reality framework of the supposer, whether seen or unseen. At this point, I do not wish to minimize the importance of recognition. To reach the permanent state of spiritual realization that underlies it all, one has to distinguish among the spiritual teachers, preachers and pretenders and those that I have gifted with the power of Ascension.

This is a point to which I return many times in these dictations. Why? Because so many have either assigned their spiritual destiny to others or they have been simply

16

misled with false hopes. Eventually, many will come face to face with those to whom the power of Ascension has been granted. If they recognize the marks of those with that gift and are adequately prepared, the gift will be granted. They will, at that moment, transcend the spiritual mind and enter MY permanent reality, whether sartori, nirvana, the void, jivan mukti or the Kingdom of Heaven.

By no means do I diminish the roles of spiritual teachers. Many are situated within MY being and do speak the truth about the spiritual life and higher realities. These teachings are important because they help people to know that there is more to life than its day to day struggles, and to hope for a better life. Yet though they may accurately describe the character and nature of Me, very few can give you direct access to Me, which you can only get via Ascension. Make no mistake, once in Me, your efforts are no longer directed at achieving Me, but they are on ignoring the downward pull of the mortal existence. As long as one has a physical body, it will act a transformer of environmental intentions, desires, etc., of the lower nature. Its grounding function is Important because few will have the luxury of being absent from some sort of physical environment and its needs. Thus, each reliably finds time for prayer, meditation, and contemplation as such, in MY being. Most find joy in extolling MY virtues and the joys of the spiritual life.

What is life like in MY permanent reality? First, one is seldom overcome by circumstances. One lives mostly within a field of love and forgiveness. Divine virtues are the hallmarks of this life. To others, one may seem to accept current conditions. To some, one may appear to be opposed to current conditions. Another may appear reactive. Yet each is operating within a Divine state of being with a viewpoint that is clear and undimmed, choosing how to function within their current reality. They mostly retain the hallmarks of their original personalities and eschew private discussion of their own Divinity. Why? Because achieving Divinity is not important enough to discuss. It is only important to Be.

Discussion by itself is limited and limiting, a further indication of the mind's inability to grasp that which cannot be grasped. Let ME be clear here. While admonitions to Be are well intended, your Being is within the human reality frame. You will see that, once you have experienced Ascension, you are truly Be—ing within MY world in a way that cannot be imagined. Indeed, some might say it is beyond their imagination and wildest dreams. How could it not be, given the inherent nature of the mind?

Free and heal yourself of your lower states in preparation for Ascension. I guarantee that once you truly experience ME via Ascension you will know that there is no comparison between what you suppose is a higher state and realization via Ascension.

My Love, surrounds, sustains and uplifts you Always.

THE TRUE MEANING OF CHRISTMAS

For several days now, many people have been celebrating Christmas. While the broad and main intention of Christmas is the recognition that a very unique Being was born, lived and was horribly crucified, as were many at that time, the recognition is not of the man himself, but of the possibility that his messages foretold. Powerfully intelligent and wise beyond his years, some might say, his goal was to present a message from and of eternity. That message, quite simply, is one of personal transformation that included the direct experience of Me, which he metaphorically described as the "Kingdom of Heaven."

Could Jesus' message have been that devils can be cast out? Could it have been that people can be healed? Could it be that miracles can be wrought? The answer to all three is No. His message was a very simple one. All of the previous activities were merely to get the attention of both the disciples and the general populace. He was quite clear about it, when he said, "The Kingdom is within." Many of you, without realizing it, exist in a pre-heavenly state quite similar to those of Jesus' time. That is, your lives are burdened and burdensome. You are weighed down with guilt, anger, depression and lack, the latter of which is a key element of modern social structure and organization. In fact, in sociology, it is recognized as the key to social stratification. This means that many people see themselves and the lives that lead as less than or more than the lives of others.

Jesus' overall intention and MY direction to him was to set in motion steps that people can take that would not only free them spiritually but, most important gain them entrance to, and residence within, Me. As such, he was uniquely vested with miraculous powers, powers that he gave directly to his disciples. The purpose of the miracles that I allowed was for people to accept him directly as MY son, which many did. Since that time many healers, prophets and spiritual teachers have come and gone. In truth, only Jesus' message remains, that being that one must accept that Jesus today forgives sin; that one may accept him as their savior and live within a state of salvation.

The capacity to erase sin is both overestimated and underestimated. It is overestimated by some that seem to believe themselves to be cured of sin, but who pride themselves as being "saved," without truly living out the opportunity that Jesus has granted and who return to the patterns of life previous to becoming saved. The underestimation of forgiveness of sin is by those outside the Christian community that fail to recognize the burdens they carry and who have no idea of the power and freedom that comes with the forgiveness of sin. It is a momentary experience, akin to Jesus' healings that he completed when he said, "Go thy way and sin no more."

What sins did Jesus have in mind when he stopped a woman's stoning?. He told the crowd, "Let him who is without sin cast the first stone." No one did. To onlookers, her sins were her lifestyle. The sins that Jesus was referring to were the sins that drove her to that lifestyle. In modern terms, it could have been early sexual and physical abuse, issues of self esteem, and so forth. I am describing her sin in ways to which you might relate. The greatest sin is not one of commission, in terms of what one does. The greatest sin is of omission of ME in your life. The greatest success is not one of achievement; it is one of inclusion within Me.

This is a point to which I will return, time and time again. When you not only "understand" this point and have accepted Ascension and committed yourself to the growth within ME that it portends, then any reading you do from here on is solely to remind yourself of what you have and are experiencing and to equip you with words and phrases to ease another's passage to and in Me.

In ancient times, what gained Jesus' acceptance as the Son of God were the many and wonderful miracles he worked. Today what needs to be accepted is the possibility of being in MY Kingdom. Some thought that would come with Jesus' physical return to earth, much like his appearances to the disciples following his crucifixion. The truth of the matter is that, as Jesus proclaimed, MY Kingdom is here and now. I have vested Gregory, with the key to MY Kingdom. He, in turn, has vested others with the key, and they, in turn, will vest others. They call themselves "light givers" and operate without a portfolio of allegiance, which is to say, they are not recruiting people to a spiritual path, organization or church. Their mission, as is Gregory's, is to be simply messengers of Light and Love, giving the Key to all those that seek it, knowing full well that those that fiercely retain their sins will be unable to share the Divine Light and It, in turn will not tolerate them.

The forgiveness of sin precedes entry into MY Kingdom. Most importantly, the forgiveness of sin requires the release and forgiveness of self. It is an internal and eternal healing that occurs. It is the completion of your spiritual journey preordained by and for you. While Christmas appears to focus on the phenomena of the man called Jesus, its true focus is on the miracle of you in MY Kingdom, which is all Jesus really wanted people to know. Jesus was born, lived and died. You are born, living and will die. This dictation is embedded with MY Holy Light. The Light Givers, to whom I have given the key to MY Kingdom, stand ready to support the completion of your spiritual journey and to share the key with you. From that point on, it is essential that you maintain your spiritual practice and yourself in Me.

I know some may reject the Christian tone of MY message. To you I say, experience Ascension in which context it best occurs for you, but if you use the Jesus Christ matrix in its terms, your amazement will be boundless, as was Gregory's, when he experienced it. He is a messenger of Light as you will be when you accept the key to MY Kingdom.

This can be done.

When you accept the Key, life will never be the same and you will truly be in MY kingdom and will share the Message and the Key with others.

THE GREAT ILLUSION OF LIFE: PRAYER

This dictation will be hard for many, especially Christians, but it is well time for it. The prayers that are made by humans today are worth nothing to me. I am not in the prayer business. I leave the business of prayers to MY Sons. Some are granted by the Holy Angels, some are granted by Jesus and some are granted by MY Son, Beelzebub, better known as Satan, the Negative Power. I ask and expect just one thing from MY human offspring and that is to narrow if not eliminate the gap that separates us.

How may a new car, job, woman, husband, healing and so forth, contribute to the elimination of gaps. In fact, most prayers are stopgaps for some material or physical insufficiency. Some may think I ignore prayers. This is not correct. I do not ignore prayers. I simply cannot hear them. Now, understand this, most humans are embedded within material reality. There is constancy of action, reactions, emotions, and a swirl of somewhat undefined needs and appetites. In fact, most are simply or nearly overcome with the power of the material world. Prayer in this context is like a drowning man gasping for air while splashing briefly through the surface of the water. A few gasps, then he is submerged again with the whirlpool of life.

To continue the metaphor, who are the lifeguards standing by, with the power to hear the last gasps and to throw a life preserver, which gives him only a momentary respite from the vicissitudes of mortality? They are MY Sons, Jesus, the Holy Angels and Satan himself. Subsequently, the preserver dissolves and once again the individual sinks below the waves. This is a drama of the individual life. What must be understood are the simple mechanics of prayer. Here's how it works. The prayer contains within it, the primary attention and intention of the praying individual. If the prayer is for a new house or car, then one's attention is on the thing and one's intention is to possess or own the automobile.

Such prayers are meaningless in MY world. But they are meaningful to MY Sons. To Jesus, some prayers are heard and granted because of the spiritual worthiness of the requester, in terms of having accepted Him as their savior and pledged themselves to preaching and teaching His gospel. The granting of such prayers is tied directly to the spiritual worthiness of the individual. How is worthiness determined? It is clearly a function of their personal spirituality. The Holy Angels likewise, take into account the worthiness of the individuals. However, they are not as rigorous in their application, being more concerned with the overall spiritual atmosphere of the planet. Thus, they may grant prayers to individuals in connection with their long-term plans for the planet.

Note, I do not indicate that they are acting, in concert, with MY long-term plans. I have none. Once I open reality in any dimension and constitute its awareness, I no longer access the field. In fact, I have no way of directly accessing the field, other than to occasionally tap into the consciousness of a Son to briefly see the world of experiences with His eyes. Let ME be clear that salvation is insufficient for entry into MY Kingdom. Although Jesus has the power to induce the Kingdom, it is only a temporary experience because of the power of the world of illusions. And most praying individuals have not renounced the lower Kingdom. Practically before the prayer has completed, the individual has once again submerged himself in the struggles of the lower Kingdom.

I am Source, known as God to Christians. MY world may not be entered. Entering is action that requires coming from and going to. You are already IN MY world. Yet you do not realize it. So, it is essential that you eliminate from your consciousness the fixations you have about your life. And to heighten your spiritual awareness. Shift your attention from the world of need to the world of haves. In that way, MY Divine essence will flow to complete. As such the Holy Angels and/or Jesus may sharpen the manifestation of MY Glory in your life. What is completely misunderstood by so many is that prayers of adoration, blessing and worship, the highest form of prayer serve only to blur, if not eliminate, the distinctions or barriers to full realization.

Now, let ME sharpen the point so that there is no misunderstanding. One's prayers for self-improvements, possessions, life partners, etc., are worthless. The only prayers of value are those of spiritual improvement. This means, quite frankly, that when you pray, you must indicate that your request is "in Jesus' name" and that whatever is being requested is in accord with MY will, so I may spread the gospel and/or so that you can achieve true realization of MY Kingdom. "True Realization" acknowledges that MY Son, Satan, has created a duplicate Kingdom to replicate the experiences that many associate with spiritual advance, such as annointing, prophecy, healing, etc. So, Satan is afoot in these situations and is firmly locking people into his Kingdom by making them think Jesus or I am granting their prayer requests.

Understand this. I am not in the prayer business. The realm in which I exist is not amenable to the actions and activity of prayer. By definition, they are manifestations within and of the Lower Kingdom, the Negative Power.

FEAR NOT

Jesus is said to have told his disciples: "Fear Not, for I am always with you." What isn't clear to most is that he was instructing them to fear Not, as in nothing. Most think he was telling them not to be afraid. The truth of the matter is that he was instructing them to fear Not or nothing. Why? Because at the heart of being human is the fear of nothing or non-existence.

So, Jesus was telling His disciples to fear the state of nothing and that the eternal consciousness in which he truly exists remains available to them. Thus, their fear of nothing compels them to be aware of the spiritual essence evoked by true Divinity. Fearing nothing or of being nothing propels the individual into a higher state of awareness separating him from the nothingness of daily life. What can be worse than being completely immersed in life's problems, so much so that sight of the eternal consciousness is lost, i.e. being lost in the nothingness of daily life, the meaningless of controversies, of actions and reactions, of wealth lost and gained, even of weight lost and gained.

This is the "not" that must be feared. It is the existence that is nonexistent or the "not" that does not truly exist. Down through the ages and even in this series, I have said over and over again that you must re-center your awareness of what is true and what is not true into MY very beingness. You cannot grip tightly onto material reality and expect to be fully aware of MY spiritual reality. Some of you may remember the story about how monkeys were trapped by hunters. The hunters simply placed fist sized groups of nuts in cages and made holes in the sides of the cages about the size of the monkeys' fist. Thus, when the monkeys filled their paws with the nuts, they were unable to withdraw because their fists were full of the nuts. So, they were trapped and easily caught by the hunters.

So it is for most humans; they are unable to withdraw into the heavenly state of existence because their grips are tightly filled with the problems, worries and treasures of material life. And, correspondingly, they are trapped by the negative power and consigned to a lifetime of want, lack and acquisition. None of this is bad of itself. This is merely how the worlds operate, designed as a test of spiritual reality.

Americans heard their president say many years ago, "We have nothing to fear, but fear itself." He was only partially correct, in that underneath concerns at the time was the basic fear that the Nazi war machine would eliminate life on the planet and substitute its own version of non-existence. Thus, the greatest fear was the elimination of life; in a way it was another version of "Fear Not," or fear of non-existence.

I will now extend the metaphor. What is the basic purpose of fear? It is to activate, propel and compel you to seek and to exist at a level outside of the fear band. The point is that you must not sustain yourself in Fear, which is at the heart of material existence, which explains the desperation that most feel and live. What fear does is give you the opportunity to catapult yourself away from what you fear, i.e. non-existence. In this instance, you are being told directly to fear non-existence and to do whatever it takes to avoid non-existence. When Jesus said, "Fear Not," he was reminding the disciples and anyone listening, including you, that for those living in the lower reality that are willing to accept his saviourship, He is the Key to eternal existence.

That is the Key that has been given to Gregory and those with whom it has been shared, whose spiritual worthiness and disciplines have brought them to the point where the Key will give them entry to the Kingdom of Heaven, far above the worlds of non-existence and Not. Fear Not. Please do not misunderstand me. There are many outside the realm of Christianity that may be spiritually worthy and for whom the Key will grant access to their heaven within our Kingdom.

However, I am directing Gregory to share the Key with the Christian community, expecting that it will rescue those being misled by false prophets, greedy preachers and pastors and others that purport to speak in MY and Jesus' name. I will speak to that crowd in a future dictation, but woe upon them because they deceive MY flock.

Indeed, they should fear non-existence because they are earning eternal non-existence on a daily basis.

GOD MESSAGE #11

SPIRITUAL VAMPIRISM

This is a message that is long overdue that I have hinted at in earlier messages. Were I human, I would say that I weary of those who would speak in MY name, those who are nothing more than spiritual vampires in that they do nothing more than drain their followers of their possessions, much as vampires drain their victims of their lifeblood. They hold themselves up as examples of God's blessings, when, in fact, they are shining examples of the Negative Power's gifts.

Here is what must be understood. There are two polarities through which individuals must transition to reach the higher worlds, whether known as sartori, jivan mukti, nirvana, kingdom of heaven, valhalla, Eckshar, the void or other names. The first polarity is that of the Negative Power that is charged to hold evolving souls in the grip of the lower consciousness or lower worlds.

The second polarity is that of the Divine consciousness that is charged to draw evolving souls in transcendence of the lower consciousness. Ultimately, this can only be done via Ascension, which occurs as a gift from one so endowed or gifted to another, or via "Sourccination," from another or the www.lightgivers.org website.

Key to this transcendence is the individual's having achieved the penultimate of his spiritual path, i.e, the release of all negativities, the forgiveness of all offenses, the elimination of all sin and past karma and the willingness to accept Ascension. In some traditions, the Negative Power is known as Kal; in others, as the Tempter or Satan.

These so-called spiritual leaders prance, parade and preen themselves in front of audiences of various sizes, providing nothing more than entertainment in the name of spirituality, hypocrites all. I use the term "spirituality" loosely because there is really nothing, read these words carefully, *nothing* about them that is spiritual. Some seek to overwhelm the audiences with their mastery of scripture; others seek to impress their audiences with their mastery of theological points. Others seek to impress their audiences with their healing and psychic abilities, or, even their access to me, when they are nothing more than recorders for disembodied entities.

Few are vibrationally linked to me. These you may recognize by their refusal to accept responsibility or ownership of the materials presented and delegate that to some higher being or non-being, like MY self. Note that I use "psychic" rather than spiritual. The abilities they demonstrate are psychic, in that they are not MY gifts, but those of the Negative Power, whose minions share bits and pieces of truth to enchant and bind listeners to their pastors, so-called prophets, so-called apostles, gurus, mahatmas, mahantas, churches, ministries and religious organizations. Often, the "prophets" preface their comments with "God is telling me," when I am not telling them anything. In fact, they are only hearing what the Negative Power wants them to say. Even the healings being done, alleged to be in MY name, are orchestrated by the Negative Power.

Now, this does not hold true for all MY messengers; some are being spoken to by Jesus or the Holy Archangels on MY behalf. But these are few and far between. The purpose of the Negative Power, which is the job I have given it, is to bind all in these lower worlds that refuse to escape via Ascension. Why would I want people to be told that they are going to receive money, get a new spouse, get that car or job that they have always wanted? Just think about it, why would I, in MY heavenly kingdom, care one whit about such earthly thing? No material or physical thing for which many will pray can be admitted to MY Kingdom. The answer is that I do not care.

In some cases, because of your commitment to spreading the word about these spiritual healing technologies, your request may be granted by the children of the Light. But, understand this: your request is only granted because of how it will help you teach others about Ascension. The only thing I care about or want is for each of MY children to be at home in the Kingdom via Ascension.

Jesus' miracles, as I have said elsewhere, were for people to accept his Divinity and the truth of his message. Today, I have released the Universal Healer, Light Giver and Rainbow Spiritual Healing technology so that the second part of the Divine message may be realized, i.e. to affirm the Divinity of every single person on the planet, if they choose. In his time, Jesus taught that the Kingdom of Heaven is within, but his mission was not to give people access to it at that time. His mission was to forgive sins, grant salvation and to prepare a place where those admitted to the Kingdom would reside.

The mission of this spiritual healing technology is to admit, via Ascension, all who accept it. Of course, forgiveness of sin, salvation, and so on are all bundled into the Ascension technology. While they may not be advertised or publicized as such, be assured that they are there. In future days, it will be incumbent upon all who witness these false prophets and deceivers to discern the sheer hypocrisy of their ministries. Many have gained great wealth by draining their followers of their possessions and, ironically, parade their belongings, cars, houses and so forth as evidence of God's generosity before the very people whose wealth has been pillaged. It would be fairer to say that what they are exhibiting are examples of the lower world's duplicity.

I call on anyone who reads or hears this message to divest themselves of their attachments to those who exhibit such Satanic connections and to realize and understand that I hear no prayers or petitions. I have delegated that responsibility to Jesus, MY Holy Archangels and the Negative Power, which allowed Jesus to declare that, if a request is made in his name, it will be granted. As a rule of thumb, if God or Jesus is not included in a request, then the Tempter or Negative Power is obligated to respond. What Jesus did not explain is that the Archangels will be dispatched to respond on His and MY behalf. What he also did not explain is that such requests must, in some way, support his mission.

Today, the message is one of Ascension. Whenever anyone brought anything to his attention that was not so aligned with this mission, he would explain that his mission was not to be a divider of things, an assigner of wealth or even to stone one that had sinned, by current standards. I leave to Jesus and the Holy Archangels the responsibility to respond to your request. If it is not in Jesus' name, then the Negative Power will respond and reserve your place in whatever form of Hell is consistent with your belief system, until you relinquish the mutual hold of the Negative Power so that you, at last, allow yourself to be completely absorbed in MY Holy Light.

THE NECESSITY OF FAITH

George Michael sang about faith to a lost love some years ago. Some of his lyrics apply. He sang:

> *Because I gotta have faith*
> *I gotta have faith*
> *Because I got to have faith, faith*
> *I gotta have faith, faith, faith*

Faith is what is required for one to move beyond uncertainty into MY kingdom. That is, you must have faith that it is possible. The precursor of faith is belief. Without believing that it is possible for you to experience the heavenly state while still in the physical body, then faith will simply not manifest.

Do you understand me, here? You must believe in the Divine possibility. Belief must penetrate your very core and radiate throughout your entire body system. Fill yourself with belief. Say over and over again, "Yes, I do believe with all MY heart." Do not move ahead and say, "I know I can enter the kingdom or Ascend." If you say that, be aware that it is your mind trying to trick you, trying to take over your personal Divine journey.

Belief quiets the mind and gives it the only tool that I have given it, and that is to open the window to MY world. And, that is the power of belief. So, settle in, allow your mind and body to be fully immersed by the power of belief. Imagine that belief is a very large ocean into which you are plunged and that every cell of your body is soaked with belief. When you feel that you are completely absorbed by Belief and that it has completely absorbed you, allow your strong feeling of belief to transform into the elevating awareness of faith.

In George Michael's song, he was letting a girlfriend know that he was reluctant to go forward with their relationship because he didn't have faith. You must be willing to go forward with your relationship by surrendering all doubts, uncertainty, hesitation and reluctances and enter into a faith relationship with Me. Now, allow the clarifying feeling of faith to replace belief. Notice how your journey now seems lighter and even more uplifting.

The way ahead now seems much clearer doesn't it? There are no obstacles in your path. All obstructions, hindrances and impediments no longer present themselves.

The power of faith transcends all earthly boundaries and establishes a golden pathway between you and the heaven worlds. Notice how faith has brought you above any and all lower boundaries. You are well on your way to the highest spiritual experience you have ever had. St. Paul wrote: "Now faith is the substance of things hoped for, the evidence of things not seen." He might well have written faith is the substance of things that are.

So, even though you may see yourself yet in the heaven worlds, there is a sense in which you already are. When you truly experience faith, you are within MY yet unmanifested kingdom. The effect to which I am bringing your attention is that faith is like the underlayment that supports a wooden floor. It is the very heart of MY essence, which sustains all that is and the core of what is being referred to when you are reminded that we are One.

It is somewhat ironic that, in order to experience Oneness, you begin within Oneness in a way that fully anticipates its destination or emergence as the true experience of Me. Yet you must experience the transition from faith through belief to knowing to being to doing. Each stage is only necessary because much of it occurs in juxtaposition to external reality and equips you each to balance that which you are experiencing with your inner experience and strengthens, holds and sustains you in ME in ways that your mentally incomprehensible, but, nevertheless, real.

The Light Givers™

2011

Dear Light Givers,

I begin sharing these Light Giver Messages with some trepidation or nervousness. Why? Because there is a great tendency these days to 1) see the message giver as a great Being, or 2) to give great importance to the message simply because it purportedly is being delivered by some invisible being(s), be they Archangels, Ascended Masters or any of a variety of extraterrestrials. What makes something true is not necessarily from whom it comes, but whether or not it is a) believable, or b) resonates within one's own consciousness.

Nevertheless, I cheerfully admit that neither the Universal Healer program that preceded the Light Giver and Ascension program nor the Light Giver and Ascension programs were MY idea. Both were given to ME by members of the Ascended Master and Archangelic Community after I was assigned the responsibility by a benevolent and well meaning and quite developed spiritual master I was following at the time. In fact, I had no idea what a Universal Healer was. When I asked, I was told, "You'll know when you write the book." To which I replied, "What book?" The answer, "The

Universal Healer." MY response, "How can I write a book about something I don't know?" The answer, "It will be dictated to you." MY response, "What's dictation?" That was seven years ago. Since that time, a 158 page book was produced, <u>The Universal Healer: A Handbook for the Advanced Healer</u> along with many dictations, seminars and quite a few Universal Healers. I now understand that the major purpose of the Universal Healer work was to lay the groundwork for the Light Giver and Ascension program.

I will also cheerfully admit that, initially, MY work was overseen by a wonderful Teacher, who has since asked to be anonymous, who is still physically embodied, who helped ME over a few bumps along the way until I could totter along at these levels pretty much on MY own and work directly with the Archangels and Ascended Masters. I will also cheerfully admit that, all claims to the contrary, our own colossal egos kept bumping into each other, so we parted ways within a year of our first association.

Rather that identifying which particular member of the Light Giver program is the author of one paragraph or another, I am simply entitling each dictation as a Light Giver Message and will leave to you the responsibility of deciding the

authenticity of the message, based on its content, not on who is designated as the particular author. OK?

Happy Reading and Happing Be-ing,

Gregory,
The Founder - The Light Giver Program

#1

THE SOURCE OF TRUE WISDOM

Dear Light Giver,

Having been Sourccinated with Multiplied Healing Light, you are now automatically generating Soul consciousness to your environment, including the people around you. If you completed the process, you are also now well established in the Soul Domain, able to be responsible for all that passes through your consciousness, free of karma and even more committed to achieving your spiritual goals.

Congratulations! We salute you.

The truth of the matter, however, is that one journey has ended and yet another journey has just begun. The journey of Soul Consciousness is one of "leaving" the lower states. The journey now is one of "Becoming" the higher state. You are now being drawn, even more so, into Source. The energies necessary to "complete" your journey are now with you. What matters is that you must now, using free will and your God-given freedom of choice, alter the paradigm by which you live. That paradigm, for most, is to see in others, such as Archangels, Ascended Masters, gurus, Satgurus, and even embodied Masters like Gregory, greater capacities than you have.

Every capacity that they have is likewise present in you. Our work with you is aimed at helping you manifest those capacities. In this message, the capacity we address is that of wisdom. Many do not see themselves as wise. So, they study the works of others, listen to their lectures and spend needless hours trying to remember what was said. Wisdom cannot be assembled from others' materials. Wisdom only emerges from within. To be sure, it can resonate, harmonize, even reflect in synchrony with others' work. But, the Source of all wisdom is the light from within. The challenge we all face is learning how to broaden and keep broadening the wisdom channel and, most importantly, to recognize and respect what comes through the wisdom channels of others.

All "wisdom" comes through one's own higher consciousness, whether basic intuition or channeled information from a higher being. Gregory knows that he is blessed to hear and think these thoughts. It is important for him to be humble and to allow these thoughts to flow through him without interference from his ego, thoughts or self-importance. It is a moment for great humility for anyone who brings such information through.

The first real purpose of the Light Givers and Ascension program is to expand others' connections to their own inner Source. You cannot be brought to the true consciousness of all, or one with All, until such expansion occurs. Unless that occurs, there is a risk of being captured by the Divine Illusion, which will be explained in a future Message, if not in the next.

So, it is important that we clear out and heal any obstacles to your directly accessing your inner wisdom and teach you how to remain clear and healed. Thus, the Auric and Soul clearings and healings of Sourccination have the mere intention of removing a few distractions and allowing you to focus on what truly matters – your complete integration into your own personal Divinity.

This will be done by your remaining in Multiplied Healing Light and accepting experiences beyond your wildest dreams and the limits of your imagination.

But let us be clear. The Light Giver and Ascension program was not created by Gregory. It was given to him as a responsibility to carry out as part of his Divine mission. In other words, we are not interested in presenting a totally new approach. What we want to do is give you a way to make your old approach work better for you.

(Please notice the use of the word "we." This is an indication that the shift from Gregory as the Source to that of the higher wisdom has occurred and Gregory is now the vehicle for what we wish to share. "We," in this discourse, is the combined intelligence of the Archangels, Ascended Masters and other Light Givers who oversee this work.)

Now, before we go another step. We ask that you not make notes, memorize or outline these messages. You will not achieve a higher state by repeating, reciting or remembering what's here. In fact, you are likely to prevent yourself from ever truly understanding what's here, if you try to memorize or recall what's said. Instead, after you finish reading this, see if you can remember only one point that struck you or seemed important. If not, no matter. Whatever is worthwhile here will embed itself in your awareness and prove useful as you move ahead. So, to repeat the ideas in the previous paragraph in a different way, the purpose of this work is to give you energetic support, through the Multiplied Healing Light, which includes Ascension. This will help you achieve the spiritual and healing goals you have already set for yourself.

You simply cannot achieve a higher state of consciousness by memorizing, reciting or repeating others' thoughts. Higher consciousness is achieved only through energetic transformation, not verbal regurgitation. To be sure, reading, listening, watching and other forms of viewing enlightened works will give one glimpses of what being in a higher state is about. But the shadow of the tree is not the tree itself, as Gregory has written elsewhere. Direct experience is the only way to reach the higher states and the Light Giver and Ascension program is solely based on the possibility of what Soul sees and is able to use via direct experience. There is a saying that, "You will see it when you believe it." In this work, we say, "Once you experience it, you know it."

It is our profound desire that you reach the highest level of consciousness and that you learn how to stay free of the lower entanglements created by the illusions of life. While there is a general sense that personal discipline may help in that direction and that you do, in fact, have the responsibility for your consciousness, it is also true that this can be facilitated by downloads of more and more Multiplied Healing Light via the Ascension process.

It is the purpose of the Light Givers and Ascension program to disseminate Multiplied Healing Light far and wide. Indeed, the very fact that you are reading this document indicates that you have already received such downloads. If that is the case, what is the true purpose of this message? The true purpose is to give your mind or mental processes sufficient material to allay the fear that somehow these downloads will alienate you from the use of the mind in ordinary ways. Nothing could be further from the truth. The mind will find that many of the aberrations that interfered with its operations in the past, such as greed, lust, anger, vanity and attachment, will be dissolved. And, it will operate at a finer, higher level than ever before.

Your mind will see things more clearly, as they really are, and not be troubled by memories of past actions, hurts, disappointments and confusions. The mind will, in fact, come to understand that it has become the God mind, no longer the tool of petty emotions, reactions, or hurtful thoughts, but has become solely focused on being the pure channel of light and love. Further, the mind will delight in the God Wisdom that is able to come through and enjoy seeing the world and others as they truly are.

Earlier, we asked that you not try to memorize, recite or regurgitate what is in this discourse. Perhaps you are now beginning to understand why. Memorization and recitation causes the mind to crystallize a transient reality and is a function of the illusionary worlds. The God mind works outside illusion and does not depend upon memory. It sees what is. Imagine that you are walking through a museum of the most beautiful and interesting things. Would you be able to truly appreciate the items immediately in front of you if you spend your time trying to remember what you last saw? This process that we are doing with you now is only a beginning, a precursor of how you will experience yourself in the total Now consciousness. In such a consciousness, which is far different from that of memory, you do not have to "remember" anything. You simply place your attention "on" it and it shows up in your awareness, full and complete. In a sense, the event, person, thing, exists already in the consciousness of God. As soon as your attention is on it, it just shows up.

We would like to say that you are developing a new skill, but, in fact, you are not. The ability is already yours. It is simply latent, which means that it is there or here, but you have not realized it yet, so it is merely undeveloped. The only way you can develop it is to use it and, believe it or not, the first way is to practice not trying to memorize what it here. Instead, after you read this discourse, simply put your attention on it and see what shows up in your consciousness, your awareness, your beingness. Simply be aware that you are loosening the hold of thinking upon your awareness, so that you are more aware of being in the God mind. Practice looking at things, knowing things, and then letting go of them to see what comes into your awareness in their place. Notice how you experience yourself. Notice how you experience others. Notice how the things of the past seek their hold on your consciousness.

Be assured that you will not develop this latent ability if you do not experiment with it.

Now, you may ask, "Given that there is so much contained within the Multiplied Healing Light Energy, why not just endow it to install the God Mind?"

Well, guess what? The God Mind, as the Super Brain, is installed within the Multiplied Healing Light. But what it cannot do is override your free will and freedom of choice. It's very much like giving you the keys to a brand new Jaguar or the keys to a beautiful new home. In each case, you have to decide to drive the car or enter the home yourself. No one can do it for you. What we can do, is fuel the car with the most powerful jet fuel available and put the most beautiful furniture, solar energy and pure water in your new home. But the universe requires that you avail yourself of what is now available to you. Once you do, then we will assist you even more.

Meditation: When you meditate or contemplate, simply say to yourself, along with whatever else you do, "I and the God mind are one. I release the hold of thinking on MY awareness so that I can experience MY true awareness." Then, go with the experience.

Waking Practice: As you go through the day, notice how you experience things. Are memories, past hurts, and other reflections of the past clouding your wisdom? Direct your God mind to reveal the Now experience. And, know, joyfully, that when you experience the Nowness of the moment, you are in the God mind. In other traditions, this was known or is known as Enlightenment.

Moving or Breathing Practice: Whether walking, breathing, exercising, or doing a moving exercise such as Tai Chi, Qi Qong or some other practice, simply say to yourself, "I am One with this. I am fully aware in this moment." Drop any thought of anything else. This may seem difficult at first, but continue.

Self Energy Test: Put your palms, facing each other about 12 inches apart. State, "This represents MY wisdom channel at 100 percent."

Ask, "Please show ME where I am today."

Your palms will move toward each other to reflect the comparative width of your wisdom channel.

Do this weekly to detect the opening of your wisdom channel.

As you do your work and/or helped work with a Light Giver or Ascension Master, the channel will widen over time.

Finally, a word about Gregory:

You can also ask Gregory inwardly to assist you. For your information, he was given "Robes" of all the orders of spiritual masters several years ago and welcomed into the orders of various higher beings. However, he fervently resists putting "Sri" in front of his name and taking the stance of a spiritual master or teacher. He believes there are enough people in that role, in his somewhat mistaken belief that it is more of a hindrance to spiritual development than a help. Any help you get from him on the inner will not be coming from Gregory personally. It's more likely one of us, his higher self or, quite possibly, your own higher self. You may write him directly at Gregory@ thelightgivers.com.

But help will be given. It may not solve your situation, but it most likely will help you get back on track.

For some it will be instant. For others, it will take a little longer. But the channel will widen. Patience is more than a virtue. It is a state of Being. Do not be in too great a rush.

What is worth learning usually does not seem easy at first. The rewards are great, if not unbelievable.

Finally, we have installed within this very message, a special download of Multiplied Healing Light. Please consider it yet another gift of many we have for you to speed you along your way.

Be still and be aware.
Thank you. Thank you. Thank you.

2

THE DIVINE ILLUSION

Dear Light Giver,

Down through the Ages, teachers, masters and other savants have made every effort to help their students and disciples come to understand that what presents itself as truth or reality is an illusion. The fact of the matter is that what presents itself is reality for the moment. What has been difficult is to help people understand that the illusion is not what they see, but rather the illusion is the belief that what they see is all of what life is about. The emphases of life are the things that impress or press upon them the most and, that who they think they are, in a human sense, is all that truly matters. The point most often made is, "You are not your body; you are not your emotions; you are not what you think you are. You are Soul, the essence of God." But what does this really mean?

When Gregory was a little boy, his world was his house, his family, his neighbors, his playmates and the people who drove or walked through his neighborhood. The idea that there were other cities and nations was something that simply did not occur to him. When he became older his focus shifted and he learned that the world was bigger and, in a sense, the center of his universe shifted to incorporate a wider perspective.

The Divine Illusion is that the center of your world is your human reality. Yes, you can be and are affected by it. Yes, your life as a human being can end at any moment. But the Divine Illusion is that you have to become detached from your life as a human. This is not exactly true, anymore than in order to drive an automobile, you have to ignore your passengers, the radio, your GPS or even your cell phone. No, what you must do is simply widen your perspective, so that, in addition to being completely and totally aware of this reality, you are simultaneously aware of a perspective that is far wider and broader than what the ordinary human consciousness can comprehend. So, the net effect of the Multiplied Healing Light is to restore your awareness to the extraordinary God consciousness.

Others have written about this and described techniques like Soul Travel, Soul Journey, and so on. In truth, it is no more complicated than widening your vision from a few feet in front of you to using binoculars to examine mountains far in the distance, all the while being aware of the presence of others and other things going on. The challenge you have, that we freely admit, is that the pull of this present reality, for some, is so great that it seems somewhat impossible to widen one's view, except for a few brief moments, whether in contemplation, meditation or in momentary reflection. This is completely understandable. And we truly salute those who take the time and make the effort to receive such insights.

There is the great story about the Master who holds his student's head under water and, after finally releasing him, asks the student, "When you were under water, what did you most want?"

To which the student replied, "Air, Master!"

The way the story goes, the Master then tells the student, "When you want God as much as you wanted air, you will have it."

Well, there's another point to the story and that is that many people live their human lives with the intensity of the student wanting air and, unfortunately, life simply cannot yield the results that are wanted. So, for many, sex, food, material possessions, status and power are sought with the passion of one wanting air. The irony is that these are simply part of the Divine Illusion, constructed and provided to sharpen one's spiritual senses and to energize eventually the thrust to the wider perspective and to shift the emphasis to eternal awareness and Beingness that is more than momentary.

And there is yet another point that can be made about the story, that being that after a time, the student came to the Master and said, "I do want God with all MY heart and Soul, just as I wanted air, when you held ME beneath the water."

The Master, in our version of the story's continuation would have said, "Yes, MY son, now you must release or let go of your desire for God, so you may now have It." He goes on to say, "By becoming One with it and seeing All from that perspective."

In that moment, the student was filled with Light given him by the Master and his seeking ceased. Note that the master filled him with Light, which is what you do as the Light Giver.

Here's the point. Nothing in this work or in any spiritual work is intended to take away your freedom of choice. The Master in the story helped the student by giving him a vivid experience that showed him the power of freedom of choice. Then, when the student was ready to receive, he was filled with Light by the Master.

Once the student made the choice to desire God strongly, the hold of the lower or earthly experiences lessened, so that the student could then accept a wider perspective and was capable of seeing the Divine Illusion and accepting the higher reality.

The Light transmitted by the Master helped stabilize the student's awareness above the clutter of the mind and daily life by clearing and healing the blockages and attachments within the student's consciousness.

Our purpose, through the Multiplied Healing Light downloads and Ascensions, is to support your efforts, by not only multiplying your healing light, but by lifting you, so to speak, into a broader vision of yourself beyond what you understand to be eternity. "Lifting" is just a metaphor for refocusing and broadening your perspective, broadening it in such a way that your experience of yourself and, indeed, the world around you loses its clutter and the clarity of your spiritual vision takes hold. The most direct way for this to occur is to become fully integrated with your higher self. This is what is given to you with the Light Giver Ascensions, specifically, the God Ascension. Not only is your wisdom channel widened, but your perspective of who you are and how you experience yourself changes. You go from experiencing yourself as a human trying to know God to God knowing the human experience.

At this point, we remind you that note taking, memorizing, recording and recitation will interfere with the benefits herein embedded. Although there are words on this page designed to entrance, if not entrain, your mental function, this Light Giver Message is itself embedded with a Multiplied Healing Light download, energetically empowered to reinforce your Soul awareness and to integrate you with your higher self. Of itself, your perspective will be broadening and your true understanding enhanced. Believe it or not, note taking or memorization will only slow the process down, instead of enhancing it, because the words create mental traps and seek to confine your understanding within the limits of the concepts.

So, once again, what is the Divine Illusion? It is the viewpoint that you must transcend this reality. No, do not worry about transcending it. Your task is to accept it as part of a shared greater reality and to become one with this reality. The spiritual rewards are great.

Thank you. Thank you.

Meditation: When you meditate or contemplate, simply say to yourself, along with whatever else you do, "I and the God mind are one. I release the hold of thinking on MY awareness so that I can experience MY self in the higher self." Then, go with the experience.

Waking Practice: As you go through the day, notice how you experience things. Are memories, past hurts, and other reflections of the past clouding your wisdom? Direct your God mind to reveal the Now experience. And, know, joyfully, that when you experience the Nowness of the moment, you are in the God mind. In other traditions, this was known or is known as Enlightenment. As many have written, "Be here, now!"

Moving or Breathing Practice: Whether walking, breathing, exercising, or doing a moving exercise such as Tai Chi, Qi Qong or some other practice, simply say to yourself, "I am One with this. I am fully aware in this moment." Drop any thought of anything else. This may seem difficult at first, but continue.

Self Energy Test: Put your palms, facing each other about 12 inches apart. State, "This represents the extent of MY integration with MY higher self at 100 percent."

Then say, "Show ME where I am now." If your hands move inward, do not be disappointed. Soon, you will be at 100 percent, especially if you are given the God Ascension.

We now install within you the Multiplied Healing Light embedded within this Message.

Thank you. Thank you. Thank you.
Love and Light,
The Light Givers

3

ON MASTERS: WHY YOU WILL NOT "FOLLOW" ANYONE IN THIS WORK

Dear Light Giver,

We deliberately chose to give the Ascension Masters their title because we do understand that when the title, "Master" is used, people tend to take notice and we do want the Light Giver and Ascension Master program to be noticed. But, let us be clear. In this context, Ascension Master simply means that the holder of the title has received a very dear endowment, actually two. The first endowment is that given to the Light Givers, i.e., to perform instant Auric clearings and healings, soul clearings and healings, and the Soul Ascension. The second endowment, unique to the Ascension Master, is that of the God Ascension and the many clearings and healings associated with that.

More important than the endowments, however, is the consciousness that opens up for the Ascension Master. We say, "opens up" because we remove the barriers between the Ascension Master's consciousness and the higher aspects of Source and merge his essence with All that is. Now, while this is, indeed, what we do, the experience of it still depends upon the active use of the freedom of choice to fully experience what is. We could also say that we "bestow" the consciousness upon the Ascension Master, but, while that might be true, it is not entirely accurate. What remains is for the individual to accept the gift and take the necessary steps to broaden the consciousness so that the perspective can be fully accepted. And, there are disciplines along the way with which the recipient must be fully conversant. Else the consciousness opened up to the recipient or candidate, as the case may be, may not be fully realized. In actuality, it all depends on the work of the candidate to maintain the consciousness.

Gregory is an excellent example. First, let's dissemble the concept of "Master." History is replete with many individuals who have worn that title. And, their biographies sometimes mention and yet gloss over the struggles through which they went before they accepted their responsibility in that role. Indeed, the emphases, more often than not, are upon the glorious way in which they exemplified love for all life and God in the human form. If the book were to be written a few years ago that truly reflected

Gregory's own biography, truth be told, it would not have said that he exemplified love for all life and God in the human form. He had many lessons to learn and attachments to divest himself of.

Our purpose here is not to embarrass him or you, but to lay bare his life, so that you will well understand that mastership and God itself are well within your reach.

Gregory grew up, a little Black boy, in a segregated St. Louis, Missouri, where African Americans (then known as Colored people) went to schools provided with inferior textbooks, were prohibited from attending theatres or eating in restaurants and whose employment was limited to certain types of jobs. Although he grew up in a segregated society, his family and community values were strong. His father, a no-nonsense stern Baptist pastor, presided over the family, along with Gregory's mother, a forgiving and loving Christian, in the best sense of the word. Two brothers and an older sister rounded out the family.

After graduating from high school, Gregory went to college briefly, dropped out to work at the St. Louis post office, where he began habits that plagued him off and on through much of his adult life, i.e., social drinking and womanizing. It is not uncommon for individuals who emerge in the spiritual life to have experienced the depths. For example, Michael Bernard Beckwith, today, a spirit-filled embodied teaching master, was a major drug dealer in his youth. And, of course, the Apostle Paul experienced a major conversion while engaged in persecuting Christians.

Throughout Gregory's life, he was on a spiritual journey. He was briefly an atheist in his early twenties; a Unitarian Universalist during his mid-twenties; a Rosicrucian in his early thirties; and a member of Eckankar in his late thirties, where he remained for over thirty years. In Eckankar, he first learned about Ascended Masters, higher worlds, and Soul Travel. He was a widely sought speaker and workshop facilitator, travelling the United States, Canada and West Africa, extolling the virtues of Soul Travel and the ECK Masters. Yet in his private life, he still grappled with his afflictions of the spirit: greed, vanity, attachment, anger and lust. These were not overcome until he was well into his sixties. At that, it took a number of personal disasters to bring him to his senses.

Gregory explains, "Things happened during an intense five-year period that took MY attention away from everything I thought was important: MY parents died, MY marriages ended, I was suspended and resigned from Eckankar and the master with whom I worked after leaving Eckankar stood by silently while the very people I had appointed to their positions ostracized me." The life he had known had ended. The only thing he had left was the spiritual life.

You may ask yourself, "Why would I ever want to follow a person like that?"
Exactly.
Because, in truth, at this stage, there is no one to "follow," except yourself.
Consider this. Gregory's experiences reduced his ego attachments to ashes. He says,

"When I really, really got it that everything had been taken away, I understood that I am truly a column of God's own stardust pretending to be human."

A column of stardust. How plain and simple is that?

So, this is the man, Gregory Scott, the founder of the Light Giver and Ascension program, warts and all. If he can be an Ascension Master, any one can, right?

Right.

And this is why we have shared the low points of Gregory's life with you. We do not desire to humiliate or embarrass Gregory or his family. But it is extremely important that neither he nor any of the other Ascension Masters be placed on pedestals. To be sure, they deserve your respect and gratitude, just as you deserve their respect and gratitude. For each of you has taken up the mantle of the Light Giver and Ascension program.

It really does not matter what your struggles have been, who you have hurt, who hurt you, what failures you have experienced or even what your successes have been. What matters is that you are willing to overcome them spiritually and accept and fulfill your spiritual destiny. And, it is to this, that we and the Multiplied Healing Light are dedicated.

Now, back to the "Master" title. We only use the titles in our written materials for and to the public. Otherwise, we ask that you know each other by your names only, with none of the "Master" this or "Master" that.

Nevertheless, we do want you to know the different types of Masters. This information may be of some use in your conversations, classes and workshops, in discussion with others.

Basically, there are thee types of Masters: those who only teach; those who transmit; those who teach and may transmit on special occasions. Based on service and devotion the masters of the Light Giver and Ascension program are empowered to transmit and Ascend all who are willing and energetically qualified, whether or not they serve or are devoted.

The Masters who only teach - They discuss, present and share the nature of enlightenment. There is no way that they could discourse so well without having been enlightened themselves. Quite often, unfortunately, they are unable to do more than review the insights and tools of enlightenment, but they do not transmit the actual energy of enlightenment themselves. Nor, for that matter are they empowered to provide Ascension. We know that, in every case, their enlightenment came at the hands, so to speak, of higher transmitting beings, a fact generally not given much attention in their own biographical renditions. Yet their words are recorded, printed and published, faithfully memorized and recited by their students and disciples. These masters are very important because they prepare individuals to think about and to accept the concepts of higher states of being. Eckhart Tolle, Michael Bernard Beckwith, Deepak Chopra and Wayne Dyer seem to be examples of these.

The Masters that transmit – These masters generally avoid discussing the nature of enlightenment, leaving to the individuals the responsibility to identify such and learn about enlightenment from other sources. Thus, their work, most often, is with people that are already serious spiritual students on one path or another that have gone as far as they can go. The instruction given by the transmitting masters is the set of techniques for clearing and healing. Their role is solely to transmit healing light. Transmitting masters will pass energies on to you, but leave to you the responsibility to make the most of them. Many of these masters work silently and quietly, appearing in one's life without explanation to transmit enlightening energies and then disappearing or quietly moving away. The great ECK Master Paul Twitchell, writes of many such encounters as he was ascending into his own mastership.

The Masters that teach and transmit on special occasions – These masters discuss, present and share the nature of enlightenment, much like the Masters who can only teach. Their transmitting, usually in the form of initiations, Shakti Pats, Deekshas, and so on, serve to magnetize their followers and disciples to their teachings and their paths. The organizations that develop around them take on an ashramic character, i.e., people rank themselves by proximity to the Master, their level of initiation and the responsibilities they perform at the Master's behest. Initiations are based unabashedly on extreme service and extraordinary devotion to the Master's mission. Buddha's successor was a man who cut off his right arm to show his devotion.

Few, if any are initiated into the highest initiations available, unless they are candidates to succeed the Master. At that, the full consciousness of the Master is not passed to his successor until it is time for the master to move on. In the meantime, while disciples and students can be vested with the power of initiation, the power to install the power of initiation is reserved solely to the Master. By no means are these observations intended to be critical. They simply explain the way things are. Examples include Sri Harold Klemp, Sri Michael Edward Owens, Choa Kok Sui, and Sri Baghavan and many of the Eastern gurus and Satgurus, Bodhisatvas, Zen Masters and Immortals.

The only restrictions faced by the Light Givers are those they impose upon themselves. Soul Ascension, God Ascension and Source Ascension are freely available, along with the various healings and clearings associated with each. And Multiplied Healing Light is provided to the full extent of your willingness and ability to receive it.

Finally, in the Light Giver and Ascension program, at this time, we ask the Light Givers I to limit their services to Sourccination. This includes helping people to better understand what each element entails and the importance of the daily spiritual practices and disciplines. We urge the Light Givers I to do no more than provide simple instruction and to make no attempts to support higher Ascensions until they are brought into the ranks of the Light Givers II – Ascension Masters by Gregory. Gregory is a fully realized teaching and Ascension Master. This means that his awareness, on occasion, blends with ours, his beingness with Source, and he is completely devoted to carrying out his assigned spiritual mission.

Once trained and endowed by Gregory, the Light Givers II – Ascension Masters can support the Source and God Ascensions. The Light Givers III – Ascension Masters are endowed to support further Ascensions. There is yet another level of Light Giver beyond Ascension Master: the Advanced Ascension Masters. From this group, once completely trained and endowed, will come those who teach and support Ascensions unto infinity consciousness. At this time, in the Light Giver program, their ranks are solely composed of those who are Master Universal Healers endowed with the infinity consciousness endowment. At this time, Gregory and we are working with them, outwardly and inwardly so they can assume the responsibilities of:

1. Discussing the Divine Reality in such a way that the recipients of such wisdom get both a mental understanding and a spiritual understanding of the higher consciousness and ways of being.
2. Transmitting Multiplied Healing Light of any magnitude where indicated and to make it available himself or via other Ascension Masters to anyone who desires it.
3. Installing the Multiplied Healing Light Endowment at any level to any energetically qualified recipient or Ascension Master without regard to service or devotion.
4. Downloading – Receive blended wisdom for the Ascended Light Givers via one or more clairvoyant skills.

For your information, two years ago we gave Gregory the spiritual mantle of a teaching master along with his transmitting duties. Freely exercising his freedom of choice, not only did he refuse to carry out our many requests, he also did not perform the self healings and clearings associated with that responsibility. Thus, his physical body was unable to accept the light we were giving it and his awful eating habits caused it to degenerate. He retired for several months to a spiritual and healing retreat in California, where on a diet of mainly raw foods, by Spring 2011, he was spiritually and physically renewed by contemplations, self healing and exercise.

Gregory's work has only just begun. We have much in store for him, as the word and work of the Light Giver program expands.

If you decide to be a Light Giver I, your responsibility anticipates those of an Ascension Master. You will endow others with instant auric healings and clearings, instant Soul healings and clearings, and the first Ascension—the Soul Ascension. You will also know how support the removal of healing blockages and, more importantly, how to keep them removed.

If you decide to take Light Giver II training, you will receive the endowment and at least three Ascensions. You may receive even more prior to becoming a Light Giver II – Ascension Master.

As a Light Giver II – Ascension Master, you will carry out with even greater competence the tasks of the Light Givers and Ascension programs. You may support God and Source Ascensions and lead a variety of workshops, group healing and clearing sessions. You also will be able to blend your Light Giver endowments with your current healing practice without losing energy from either application. Moreover, depending on their backgrounds and experience, some individuals may receive the endowments, the Light Giver II - Ascension Master training and the Light Giver III – Ascension Master training on the same day. We have a great need to field as many as possible.

In the meantime, we do not wish to overload your energy field and will work with you closely to ensure that you do not receive more than you can handle. But much will be given and much will be received.

Much Love and Light,
The Light Givers
Thank you. Thank you. Thank you.

Meditation: When you meditate or contemplate, simply say to yourself, along with whatever else you do, "I and the God mind are one. I release the hold of thinking on MY awareness so that I can experience MY self in the higher self." Then, go with the experience.

Waking Practice: As you go through the day, notice how you experience things. Are memories, past hurts, and other reflections of the past clouding your wisdom? Direct your God mind to reveal the Now experience. And, know, joyfully, that when you experience the Nowness of the moment, you are in the God mind. In other traditions, this was known or is known as Enlightenment. As many have written, "Be here, now!"

Moving or Breathing Practice: Whether walking, breathing, exercising, or doing a moving exercise such as Tai Chi, Qi Qong or some other practice, simply say to yourself, "I am One with this. I am fully aware in this moment." Drop any thought of anything else. This may seem difficult at first, but continue.

Self Energy Test: Put your palms, facing each other about 12 inches apart. State, "This represents the extent of MY alignment with the Light Giver consciousness at 100 percent."

Then say, "Show ME where I am now." If your hands move inward, do not be disappointed. Soon, you will be at 100 percent, especially if you are given the God Ascension and accepted into the Advanced Giver Circle.

We now install within you the Multiplied Healing Light embedded within this Message.

4

UNDERSTANDING SOURCCINATION

Dear One,

This letter is written to give you a better understanding of Sourccination, how it works, and a simple procedure to use in Sourccination sessions, individually or with a group.

What is often difficult for many to understand is that Sourccination is a completely different healing paradigm from that with which most people are familiar. In the traditional healing modalities, the healer plays a significant role, or is presumed to. He is believed to "perform" the healing and the results of his work are understood to be the product of his efforts. In truth, whatever healing is performed is the direct result of the alignment of the recipient of the healing and the higher healing beings such as Archangels, Ascended Masters and, in some cases, groups of extraterrestrials. There is a sense in which the exercise of healing as traditionally understood is one of ego lessons for the healer and the healee. The lesson is one of surrender. The healee seems to surrender responsibility for his own healing to the healer. In turn, the healer feels some responsibility, in many cases, for the results of the healing. The healing lesson for each is not surrender to each other, but surrender to the higher power, whether it's understood to be the higher self, Jesus, Allah, Mohammad or simply Source. The little self, in both cases must step aside.

The form the healer's surrender takes is dependent upon the particular healing modality in which he is trained. In some traditions, healing is presumed to occur as a function of channeling and transmitting. In these cases, the healer is presumed to be a vehicle for the healing energy and allowing it to flow through his body to the healee. In other cases, the healer is either an invoker or an evoker. In these cases, the healing energy is invoked, in terms of flowing directly into the healee from the healing source without flowing through the invoker. Or, the healing energy is caused to emerge from within the healee in harmony with the intention of the healer.

Sourccination may be the true healing paradigm. In Sourccination all healing energy experienced by healees is coming directly from within the energy or quantum field of the healee.

What is not well known, all appearances to the contrary, is that so-called lightning strikes are really not strikes at all. In fact, they are lightning releases, in terms of being the transmission of billions of electrons from the earth upward. The truth of the matter is that the earth's magnetic field harbors trillions of electrons that are released during lightning strikes. So, even though it appears that the lightning is coming from above, in fact the lightning is coming from the earth.

By the same token, despite the appearance of healing being external to the individual, the fact of the matter is that the healing energy is truly coming from within the individual's own energy field. Why is this important to understand? It helps explain how and why Sourccination occurs as it does, in that the Sourccination process is one that releases successive layers of healing energy and awareness that the individual already has available to him, but is inaccessible for reasons related to spiritual blockages and the lack of a key to open the gateway to deeper, higher or more expanded fields of consciousness. While the hindrance posed by spiritual blockages makes perfect sense, the idea of a gateway needs further explanation.

It is generally well known that atomic fission is caused by the movement of electrons to rings further out from the nucleus of atoms of fissionable material. The simple movement of the electrons releases enormous energy. In a somewhat inverse way, the expansion or movement of consciousness associated with Ascension requires a slight infusion of energy from the Light Giver that opens the gateways of the recipient. Once the gateway is opened by the Light Giver, so endowed with what could be called an energetic key, in a metaphorical sense, the flood of energy released, if accepted, simply lifts the recipient into a higher state. To continue the atomic metaphor, as the atom is surrounded by layers of energy, Ascensions can occur through multiple layers of Awareness, far beyond those of what this work calls the Soul, God and Source Ascensions. Once the Source Ascension has been received, then the use of nomenclature stops because the individual is expanding even further into the worlds, universes and domains of even Greater Beingness, that of the nameless worlds. The Light Giver or any master so endowed performs this service without a strong intention or thought. The simple realization that the experience of Sourccination is wished or permitted by the recipient is sufficient.

Thus, in the presence of the Light Giver, the recipient has but to agree to the following, in regard to any and all spiritual blockages and to the replacing of all dark or negative energies with Divine Multiplied Healing Light. There are seven simple requests (to one's higher power, Source or spiritual guide). Whether or not the recipient is taught how to calibrate his own energy is solely at the discretion of the Light Giver. However, no one unable to calibrate energy will be admitted to the ranks of the Light Givers – Ascension Masters, for obvious reasons. S/He must know how to support the removal of spiritual blockages, and more importantly, how to keep them removed. It's that simple.

Auric Clearing and Healing

They can be as stated below or simply "Please remove":

1. I ask for the removal of any and all inhibiting beliefs.
2. I ask for the removals of any and all beliefs that enable inhibiting beliefs and any and all blockages.
3. I ask for the removal of any and all agreements, made by ME or anyone on MY behalf that have resulted in blockages to MY physical health and spiritual evolution.
4. I ask for the removal of any and all connections to others, not of light and love, that have resulted in blockages to MY physical health and spiritual evolution.
5. I ask for the removal of any and all beings, not of light and love, inside and outside MY aura, that have resulted in blockages to MY physical health and spiritual evolution.
6. I ask for the removal of any and all connections to others, not of light and love that have resulted in blockages to MY physical health and spiritual evolution.
7. I ask for the removal all influences from the past that have resulted in blockages to MY physical health and spiritual evolution.
8. Finally, I ask to be forgiven by all those that I may have offended, knowingly, or unknowingly; I forgive all those who may have offended ME knowingly or unknowingly; and, lastly, I forgive MY self.
9. I also ask that I be surrounded by a shield of Divine Healing Light that is calibrated to be impenetrable by all negative energies, forces and beings.

Explain that it is important to make these requests twice daily. Before going to bed and upon arising the following morning because negatives sometimes attack in the dream state, if the aura opens during sleep.

Soul Ascension, Clearing and Healing

Soul Clearing and Healing
This may be done in the following manner:

1. The Light Giver says: You are now Ascended
2. State:

   a. Your Life contract is now at 100 percent alignment (on a scale of zero to 100 %)
   b. Your capacity to receive God Love is at 100 %
   c. Your capacity to give God Love is at 100%
   d. You are Integrated with Divine Will at 100%

3. State: If any of these have not occurred, we now ask that all energies blocking be removed and replaced with Divine Multiplied Healing Light calibrated to bring you to 100 %.
4. State: You are now in the state of Jivan Mukti, Nirvana, the Atma Plane, Sartori, Eckshar, the Void and the Kingdom of Heaven, as identified by several religious paths. This state cannot be maintained without diligent use and application of the spiritual disciplines, such as meditation, contemplation, Tai Chi, Yoga, etc., that you already know.
5. State: We recommend that you practice blessing Source and your spiritual path on a daily basis. Blessing to the Light Givers is also recommended, as well. In each case, you will receive multiplied blessings continuously.

5

THE ART OF SURRENDER

Dear One,

In this letter, we will consider with you the question of self-surrender, which is a focus of many spiritual teachings. The general approach is that individual's difficulties in life may be resolved by learning the art of surrender. The learning of this skill usually begins with developing the art of "surrendering to the teacher." In such situations, when confronted with burdensome experiences, the spiritual student is counseled to turn his problem over to the teacher.

Stories abound in many spiritual traditions about the role the teacher plays in the student's life by helping them with their problems. In some cases, the students have inner conversations with their teacher; in other cases, they are simply aware of passing the problems over to the teacher; and, in still others, the students simply give up in the knowledge that somehow the teacher will handle the problem.

The weakness in this approach is that unless fully understood, a spiritual dependency is not only developed, but is perpetuated. So much so, that the individual lives pretty much an unsurrendered life from which he shifts into surrendering when the consequences of being unsurrendered surround or overwhelm him. Once surrendering performs its spiritual magic, then the individual once more reverts to a state of unsurrender.

What is poorly understood is that the refuge the teacher offers is intended to be a temporary one, one in which the individual has the experience of giving up the need, the hold, the attachment and, indeed, the necessity to direct a desired consequence. The lesson to be learned is not in the acceptance by the master of the individual's troubles. Quite frankly, if the consequence of MY surrendering is to know that it is now in the master's hands, it could be said that I have still directed a desired consequence of MY action or release.

In effect, there are two actions: first is MY surrendering or letting it go; the second is the knowing transference to the master. The lesson is in the surrender, not the knowing that the master now has the problem or issue. At the very instant of letting go, the spirituality of the moment has occurred. In that moment, the individual is truly free. No attention at all needs to be placed on where the issue has been bestowed, accepted or given. While such attention may not bind the individual to the issue, the bond to the master remains firmly in place and spiritual freedom as such cannot be fully known with bonds of any type.

The same risk applies to those who, in good faith, believe that they have turned their issue over to God. Most will agree that such should not be done by willing the action, or even praying for some action or result from God. Likewise, the individual must become one with the release or moment of surrender, knowing that it is not his responsibility to dictate an outcome. The true surrender is in the moment of surrender, not in the satisfaction of knowing that it is in the master's hands or in God's hands.

Most, however, seek to recreate the experience of passing the problem off. So, it becomes a "How did I do this last time, let's do it again this time. It should work, right?"

Wrong, surrender repeated does not bring spiritual freedom. The mere repetition assures spiritual bondage, if only to the technique, and the belief or hope that it will be handled. Spiritual evolution follows a spiral path, which means that no action can or should be repeated. Thus, the individual may begin surrendering to the Master. There follows learning how to surrender without regard to establishing the issue, problem or concern with the master. There follows learning how to be in a surrendered state, where surrendering is not an action but simply a way of being. This is not to say that the transition from one state to the other occurs within a moment, but it is important to know that the art of surrender has transitional phases.

It is also important to know that, along the way, a fundamental shift occurs. The individual transitions from focusing on surrendering from whatever is the focus to surrendering to his personal divinity. The issue is no longer paramount in his awareness. Instead, what is paramount is his preoccupation or relocation into his higher awareness, Soul consciousness, personal divinity, however it is known in his spiritual tradition.

Spiritual surrender should be like the experience of slowly entering a swimming pool of increasing depth. As you move into it, you are aware of being gradually covered, beginning at the ankle level. As you continue to enter the pool, the water comes up to your hips, then your chest, your face, until at last you are totally submerged. So should it also be in regard to self-surrender. Your entry and experience of it is gradual but continuous until you are fully covered and, most importantly, fully surrendered.

At this point, we remind you that note taking, memorizing, recording and recitation will interfere with the benefits herein embedded. Although there are words on this page designed to entrance, if not entrain, your mental function, this Light Giver Message is itself embedded with a Multiplied Healing Light download, energetically empowered to reinforce your Soul awareness and to integrate you with your higher self. Of itself, your perspective will be broadening and your true understanding enhanced. Believe it or not, note taking or memorization will only slow the process down, instead of enhancing it, because the words create mental traps and seek to confine your understanding within the limits of the concepts.

So, once again, what is the Divine Illusion? It is the viewpoint that you must transcend this reality. No, do not worry about transcending it. Your task is to accept it as part of a shared greater reality and to become one with this reality. The spiritual rewards are great.

Thank you. Thank you.

Meditation: When you meditate or contemplate, simply say to yourself, along with whatever else you do, "I and the God mind are one. I release the hold of thinking on MY awareness so that I can experience MY self in the higher self." Then, go with the experience.

Waking Practice: As you go through the day, notice how you experience things. Are memories, past hurts, and other reflections of the past clouding your wisdom? Direct your God mind to reveal the Now experience. And, know, joyfully, that when you experience the Nowness of the moment, you are in the God mind. In other traditions, this was known or is known as Enlightenment. As many have written, "Be here, now!"

Moving or Breathing Practice: Whether walking, breathing, exercising, or doing a moving exercise such as Tai Chi, Qi Qong or some other practice, simply say to yourself, "I am One with this. I am fully aware in this moment." Drop any thought of anything else. This may seem difficult at first, but continue.

Self Energy Test: Put your palms, facing each other about 12 inches apart. State, "This represents the extent of MY integration with MY higher self at 100 percent."

Then say, "Show ME where I am now." If your hands move inward, do not be disappointed. Soon, you will be at 100 percent, especially if you are given the God Ascension.

We now install within you the Multiplied Healing Light embedded within this Message.

Thank you. Thank you. Thank you.
Love and Light,
The Light Givers

6

THE IMPORTANCE OF SPIRITUAL PRACTICE

Dear One,

In each of the preceding messages, we have emphasized the importance of your spiritual disciplines. If you have come this far, it is no doubt because of the disciplines that you already exercise. We are writing to reinforce their importance and to remind you that you seriously must do them regularly. Now, by no means are we suggesting that you should spend many hours in contemplation or doing moving meditation. No, what we are telling you is that daily practice is essential. Why? you may ask.

The reason is quite simple. You live in a world of many invasive energies. While you are reading this, you are being constantly bombarded with billions of electronic signals: satellites from above, GPS and cellphones from all around, televisions, microwaves, automobile and television remotes, computers, refrigerator, lights, the electric sockets in your house and even your toaster. In addition, we are all energetically connected to every living thing in our environment. So, when a limb or flower is trimmed outside your home or even the grass is cut, a wave of pain goes out and though we may not feel it, believe us, it is not only registered within your energy field, but the entire universe records it. Add to this the emotions of everyone within your neighborhood, your community, and even your city.

Thus, the necessity of spiritual practices serves to balance, if not resist the avalanche of externally generated energies. Aside from these energies, there are the powerful thought forms of the external society: the images, the concepts, the paradigms, all of which are embedded with energies to make us buy, hate, fear, love, want and every other imaginable emotion.

But aside from building a power wall of protection against outside invasive energy, what are the benefits of our spiritual practice. Clearly, we are resisting what we are not. What must be emphasized and what is enhanced by our spiritual practice is what and who we are, spiritual beings vested with all the consciousness of the higher worlds, divine light beings, God incarnate. Our spiritual practice has the central aim of bringing us even more so into the full awareness of our personal divinity, so that we can be truly in this world and not of it. Maintaining this awareness is the promise Ascension offers.

In some traditions, it is spoken of as the bliss state, nirvana, sartori, Jivan mukti, the kingdom of heaven, the Eckshar, and so on. What is trying to be described is the way in which one experiences oneself, once he has become free of the worlds of causation, effects and consequences. In that world, one often is quite reactive, defensive and sometimes offensive. What is not clear to many is that, in that state of consciousness, there is a fear of non-survival. So, individual reactions have beneath them an underlying concern that somehow, unless a defense is mounted, non-survival will occur.

Spiritual practice, particularly, the arts of smiling, laughing, and blessing bring with them a fullness of life, a full awareness that one lives truly in the eternal consciousness, fully immortal, completely free and fully of life. The spiritual disciplines are essential to maintaining this awareness and must be practiced regularly if one wishes to remain in the Ascended state.

At this point, we remind you that note taking, memorizing, recording and recitation will interfere with the benefits herein embedded. Although there are words on this page designed to entrance, if not entrain, your mental function, this Light Giver Message is itself embedded with a Multiplied Healing Light download, energetically empowered to reinforce your Soul awareness and to integrate you with your higher self. Of itself, your perspective will be broadening and your true understanding enhanced. Believe it or not, note taking or memorization will only slow the process down, instead of enhancing it, because the words create mental traps and seek to confine your understanding within the limits of the concepts.

So, once again, what is the Divine Illusion? It is the viewpoint that you must transcend this reality. No, do not worry about transcending it. Your task is to accept it as part of a shared greater reality and to become one with this reality. The spiritual rewards are great.

Thank you. Thank you.

Meditation: When you meditate or contemplate, simply say to yourself, along with whatever else you do, "I and the God mind are one. I release the hold of thinking on MY awareness so that I can experience MY self in the higher self." Then, go with the experience.

Waking Practice: As you go through the day, notice how you experience things. Are memories, past hurts, and other reflections of the past clouding your wisdom? Direct your God mind to reveal the Now experience. And, know, joyfully, that when you experience the Nowness of the moment, you are in the God mind. In other traditions, this was known or is known as Enlightenment. As many have written, "Be here, now!"

Moving or Breathing Practice: Whether walking, breathing, exercising, or doing a moving exercise such as Tai Chi, Qi Qong or some other practice, simply say to yourself, "I am One with this. I am fully aware in this moment." Drop any thought of anything else. This may seem difficult at first, but continue.

Self Energy Test: Put your palms, facing each other about 12 inches apart. State, "This represents the extent of MY integration with MY higher self at 100 percent."

Then say, "Show ME where I am now." If your hands move inward, do not be disappointed. Soon, you will be at 100 percent, especially if you are given the God Ascension.

We now install within you the Multiplied Healing Light embedded within this Message.

Thank you. Thank you. Thank you.
Love and Light,
The Light Givers

THE ROLE OF THE SPIRITUAL MASTER

Dear Friend,

The thought of MY accepting apprentice masters has triggered a reaction among the Brotherhood, and within ME that opened the long awaited gateway for a flood of information now to come your way on a variety of topics. This is the first of six letters written directly to you that is the third in the Letters to Light Giver III - Ascension Master series. Hopefully, you will better understand what we are about in this work, The Light Giver. And, in sharing them with those who are accepted in the Light Giver - Ascension Master training, the expectation is that they will be able to move more fully and more comfortably into their mastership. I hope we will be able to discuss these as time goes by, and in so doing, the dialogue will harmonize the God wisdom that abides within you in such a way that you and these spirituals embed themselves and express authentically as part of your own wisdom field. Each of these letters is embedded with units of source energy to facilitate the transformation.

In this letter, I discuss to some extent, the role of the teacher or spiritual master with the expectation that you will gain a sense of not only MY perspective, but how you might consider the role into which you are being transformed.

We, in the ancient orders, have, over the centuries, established individuals in the role of teachers and spiritual masters. This is because there must be someone in the culture or group who is able to demonstrate to others gateways to higher states of being. Also, these individuals have often been the purveyors of more advanced technologies. So, the teachers would be embedded with principles, practices, and knowledge designed and intended to open their students and followers to the larger possibilities of life, and of themselves as well. And, we generally installed within the teacher endowments that would allow them to accelerate the spiritual development of some of the members of their flock.

The endowments would be of various types. They might be a string of words, such as Jesus' parables or stories. They might be healings, i.e., the simple removal of physical blockages that are replaced with healing energies. They might be upliftments such as initiations, shakti pats, deekshas and so on that give the recipient the feeling of grace, gratitude and exposure to one's own spiritual potential that awaits beyond the worlds of causation and effects.

Ascension experiences were provided far less frequently. This was done on a very selective basis, most often limited to the teacher's spiritual successor who had demonstrated, in some way, his spiritual sufficiency to receive the master's mantle and to carry the teachings on. Why? Because the spiritual freedom that accompanies the mantle can be fundamentally liberating and weaken any sense of obligation. Without a commitment to carry the work on, the path might wither and disappear. Also, many people were more interested in the form of the teaching rather than its reality or practice. There own association with the master substituted for the God devotion that was required. Such endowments in the consciousness of those that did not fully embrace the breadth of the teachings would be dangerous, indeed.

This could explain the reasons why many "men of God" sometimes abused or took advantage of their followers and incurred spiritual lessons that took them through many lifetimes of redemption. It is truly a violation of spiritual law to use spiritual endowments to trap and confine individuals for personal aggrandizement or sexual abuse. Ironically, it is now we who punish the violators. In fact, it is the Soul consciousness of the individual himself that metes out the punishment, as it were, in order to bring the individual into alignment with Source. How long does it take? As long as it takes. The egoism and callousness that allowed the misuse of the endowment must be neutralized and expunged from the energy fields of those who misuse their spiritual power.

So, the true teacher is the higher consciousness that recognizes and directs the spiritual evolution of the individual by moving him between and among their various spiritual paths or energies within his spiritual environment. Within modern society, however, individuals are inculcated to believe that true wisdom lies outside them and, therefore, often look to those with degrees, certifications, and other measures of class attendance, as sources of spiritual wisdom. In most cases, the wisdom they profess is that which has been gleaned from others' works and not wisdom they have directly accessed from spiritual beings or Spirit themselves. So, it is as if the students are in rehearsal for God whenever God chooses to show up. Quite frankly, this is good. Because when "God shows up" as God energy, the individual is more likely to be able to sustain himself in it, only if any and all spiritual blockages have been removed.

Why is the removal of spiritual blockages important? This is important because as long as the blockages are present, between moments of exultation as in contemplation, the individual will be drawn inexorably to the lower states of awareness. Until karma has been removed and a true state of spiritual freedom has been entered, God, as such, remains an aspiration, an intention, and, largely, a figment of one's imagination.

We who serve as outer teachers are sometimes characterized as Way showers. As such, we can enlighten, which is to demonstrate ways to consider, think about, and reflect upon spiritual truths in ways that allow your inner light to see light in places you may not have noticed. But I and you are Light Givers. I am endowed with, and have endowed you with the power to help unlock greater levels of inner light within others once they have accepted the removal of their spiritual blockages that occurs with the auric clearings and healings, the soul clearings and healings. These are activated by your very presence. If they do not fully occur, then the Light Giver's duty, if requested, is to lead the individual through the clearing and healing process with the seven simple questions. No intention is required.

In the orbit of a teacher, there is always the risk of overattachment to the teacher and the transference of your power to the teacher In the illusion that the teacher is transferring his power to you. While a teacher can and often does activate a greater capacity for spiritual awareness, such does not require surrender or giving up to the master. The only "giving up" should be to Source or God itself. When the Master says, "I am always with you, talk to ME on the inner," it creates what should only be a momentary experience of union leading to spiritual freedom. It is the same as if you want to go over a wall and a close friend says, "Here, step into MY hands, and I will lift you to the top". But you don't expect to spend the rest of your life with your friend attached to the bottom of your shoes. By the same token, you want to be aware of masters that wish to be in the same role for the rest of your incarnation. The lift should be into a better relationship with God, not further dependence on the master.

More Later,
Gregory

2

IS BEING FREE OF KARMA NECESSARY FOR SPIRITUAL EVOLUTION?

Dear Light Giver,

In many spiritual teachings, there is an emphasis on karma. In some, there is the idea that it is practically inescapable. More recently, the idea that one can become free of karma in a single lifetime is becoming more prominent. In either case, it is generally understood that karma is the vehicle for the spiritual training of the individual. What training one might ask? In fact, the universe is well populated with sentient beings whose primary responsibility is to manage selected aspects of its functions. This must be carried out with the proper exercise of attention and use of spiritual energy, in whatever form it appears. The very last thing these individuals can do is to be swept up or away by energetic distortions or aberrations. Karma is simply the result of the misapplication of spiritual energy that results in excess that must be either neutralized, deleted or balanced.

So, becoming free of the tendency to generate excess and/or aberrated energy is a necessary condition for spiritual advancement. Advancement to what, you might ask? Advancement to being completely integrated in full consciousness into that which we know as Source. The ultimate ambition is to be able to be individuated but solely consumed by and full of God energy. When karma is eliminated, the polarity and attraction to lower states of being vanishes and the individual is repolarized to Source. This makes possible the entry into hitherto unknown levels of awareness.

The great illusion is that, once one is free of karma, he can never create karma again. This is not true. Karma can be removed by a spiritual master so endowed that, in the time it takes to blink, it can be dissolved. But the power to create karma still remains and the karma creating machinery, as such, goes immediately to work.

What is the "Karma creating machinery?" It is the remaining imbalance in the individual's field that produced the excess, aberrated energy. Only when an individual has come into balance fully and completely can the machinery be stilled. This balance is the direct result of the individual's own application of spiritual principles and his willingness to surrender to his higher self and spiritual goals via the life contract, God energy interaction, and Soul, God and Source Ascensions. Once these have occurred, the excess energies have become completely transformed into God energy. So, it is an easy task for a master so endowed to complete the cancellation of karma creation. In this way, the individual that maintains his spiritual practices will be able to continue his spiritual evolution without the interference of spiritual blockages and excess energies, better known as karma.

If the master removes the karma creating ability prematurely, there is a risk of emotional complications occurring. These could appear in the form of excess egoism or conversely great feelings of unworthiness. So, great care and caution must be exercised by the master. You have come this far because of your love, devotion and great work in Spirit and have truly earned your freedom from karma.

Thus, you now have the power of Ascension, which, after supporting the removal of spiritual blockages from individuals, is simply unlocking the gateway to a higher state of awareness, which they must move through, in their own volition.

Finally, you will notice less of a tendency to focus on the attributes of the God State. They will begin to present themselves when circumstances call for them, i.e. humility, gratitude, grace, truthfulness, etc.

More Later,
Gregory

3

BEING THE SPIRITUAL MASTER

Dear Light Giver,

We want you to understand that your master training in this lifetime has truly begun. In this incarnation, it is occurring under the framework of your becoming the Light Giver III - Ascension Master.

As the spiritual master, you will come to understand what it means to be in this world but not of it. You will learn how to keep your consciousness fully in God and actively live the life of a human being. What is seldom understood is that the higher beings, such as the Ascended Masters, Archangels, and other God beings such as Jesus, Buddha and the many spiritual teachers that have populated this planet and others truly lived as mortals among men. This means that many of the same cares and worries we have today about our children, grandchildren and friends, were theirs, too. They had to learn the art of balancing their quite often secret passion for God with the demands of daily life. They learned how to intermingle the passions of the flesh, of love, trust, hope and honor, with their burning desire to live the God-filled life. Some went into the forests, caves and even the desert. Others stayed with their families, their villages, their communities and their kin. What is seldom known is that no matter which choice they made, as their incarnations progressed they experienced all the varieties of living arrangements, with each intended to solidify even more so the God connection.

So, there are some who discover aspects of spiritual mastery in isolation, some who come to a fuller understanding in group and, of course, some who are able to combine isolation and group. How they discover it is less important. What is important is what they do discover. Most important is where they discover it. And that is on the inner, in the inner worlds of reality. Without lapsing into rhapsodizing about the ecstatic states of awareness, know that what is discovered is the essential Beingness of God. It is a sense of personal authority over one's own Beingness and a way of seeing the world and others in it that transcends the fearful, reactive, somewhat dependent state in which many humans are.

Many people live in perpetual fear: of auto accidents, plane crashes, infection, crime, rape, lack of love, disease, cancer, etc. Underneath those fears, is the fundamental fear of death or non-survival. The spiritual master, while knowing that caution needs to be exercised in many situations, has no fear of non-survival. He knows that he lives in the eternal consciousness and, as such, is an immortal being. When the body stops, he knows he will move out of it, consult with the higher self and those higher beings that have been overseeing his progress, and take on his next incarnation, be it on earth or elsewhere in the universe in service to God, as a human being, Ascended Master, Archangel, Extraterrestrial, Deity, Time Lord or some other sentient being.

What motivates such fearlessness is the direct experience of Source, which is the ever expanding absorption into Spirit and its field of Love and the eternal consciousness.

This is an awareness that must be gained directly through one's spiritual practice of full absorption and immersion in Divine Light and Love. There are a few techniques to be shared that will deepen and accelerate this immersion.

More Later,
Gregory

4

THE TRUTH ABOUT SPIRITUAL DETACHMENT

Dear friend,

In this letter, I discuss the true secret of detachment. Detachment is well known within the spiritual works as an aspect of higher consciousness. For many, it is thought to be a sense of distancing from outer circumstances. In fact, some seem to regard it as a prize of spiritual consciousness and believe that one is to live largely unaffected by outside circumstances. What is poorly understood is that the emphasis of detachment has absolutely no relationship at all with outer circumstances. One does not pick and choose that with which he will be affected. One does not or cannot look at the stream of life and decide I will be affected by that and I will not be affected by this. Such an understanding of detachment is fundamentally incorrect. So, the idea of non-attachment also is off the mark. Once again, the individual who is attempting to live the non-attached life is missing the mark.

What is at the heart of understanding this spiritual stage is knowing that what is at issue is the true nature of spiritual polarity. Spiritual polarity relates to what is the fundamental attractive power in the individual's life. Is the individual fundamentally drawn to the worlds of causation and effects or is the individual fundamentally attracted to the Source world? It's not a matter of what's important, what the individual thinks is important or what others think is important. It is directly related to the individual's own Beingness, his essential nature. Thus non-attachment and detachment are two faces of the same coin, the coin of attachment. Why? Because their essential reference is to something outside themselves well located in the polarity of causation and effects. With non-attachment, there is sometimes a feeling of superiority because nothing is said to affect the individual. Likewise with detachment, the individual selectively diminishes his reaction to some outside event. But in both cases, the outside events are the primary referents. Please do not misunderstand me. Being aware of these states of being are good and important referents as one moves into the higher states, but they must be temporary referents and impermanent.

So, what is the true state in which one must exist? That state is complete God absorption. Thus, when one chants, I am one with God or speaks of being within the

God mind, one is acknowledging the possibility. The limitation of this perspective is that, for most, it is at best a strongly held belief, one of conviction. Unfortunately, it cannot be achieved or known until the spiritual blockages are removed. These hold one in or force the return to the worlds of polarity, much like ballast on an aerial balloon. So, with the ballast in place, the detached or non-attached individual is like a man standing on a mountain top wondering about the power of flight as he sees birds soaring about him.

It makes no more sense to believe one can be genuinely unaffected by what goes on around him than one can assume that tissue paper placed in water will stay dry. How can one even imagine that the individual holding God consciousness can see life as it is and not feel love, compassion, mercy, kindness and the many other God virtues of spirit? What must be understood is that God consciousness allows the individual to fully understand and experience all dimensions of life in full context. And what is that context? The context is that all is of God; all is God in expression in action.

Thus, it is a contradiction to even imagine that God is unattached. God is attached to all. How could it not be? What underlies all considerations of attachment and non-attachment is the fear of extinction or, at least, of being overwhelmed by events. With the full awareness and experience of one's own God-absorbed immortality, the fear vanishes. Thus, one can cheer at sports events, laugh and cry at movies, experience great tender love and powerful sex and know, in his heart, that nothing can truly overwhelm more than the fullest expressions of God, i.e. full absorption.

More Later,
Gregory

5

THE NECESSITY OF LOVE

Dear friend,

In this letter, I write about the sheer necessity of love. Love is the very essence of all life. Quite simply, it is the glue that binds the entire universe together. This is not a romantic love. This is not a magnetic love. In fact, as we experience it here on earth, it is only a pale reflection of its true essence. Yet how we experience it gives us a sense of what it is in the higher reaches of the universe or in the heart of god. It is the divine force to which one must surrender oneself and for which one must become a solid beacon of light. As the human, we are given many experiences to allow us to appreciate it in all of its nuances: Strong, Weak, Slightly, Totally and Completely. What must be understood, however, is that nothing we experience here on earth bares even the slightest resemblance to what is experienced in the heart of Source. Not even one who has reached many of the exalted heights of spiritual experiences has even come close to its fullest awareness. One reason is that, in the ultimate full awareness, it is quite possible to lose one's sense of the individuated self and the capacity to relocate within the "body of God."

In the fullest awareness of God, there is not only immortality but there is in a sense, immobility. If God is everywhere, then it cannot move. To be sure, there appears to be some transient awareness of momentary experience, but, in truth, God cannot and does not "see" in the way that we think of such seeing. Once I was given the experience of being at one with its totality. What I became aware of was that there were dimensions of MY self in which I was not fully present and that there was a need for MY presence to be fully extended or represented in those areas. At that, I am now fully aware that there was an even greater knowledge and awareness that more than transcended, if not eclipsed, the consciousness needing expansion. It is almost as if the consciousness that needed expansion was MY body and the greater consciousness is that which was aware of the areas in which MY body needed to be expanded or made denser. There was no place in the universe in which I was not, but some areas were less dense than others.

The feeling that accompanied this awareness of two levels is one of such ultimate compassion and completion that even to say it is transcendent is an understatement.

This underscores the value of using contemplative techniques in order to become even more translucent to the Divine power. This knowledge then needs to inform the active contemplator in ways that he invests more of his attention on full absorption into and by the God power and full attention on the Godliness of all experience, on living life in the full wonder and excitement of freeing himself of energy entanglements, while begrudging no one his love.

The challenge that we face in the human embodiment is that we are under siege by energy intrusions of many types. These range from food poisoned with pesticides, to emotional entanglements by friends and loved ones, to energy pollution of electronic devices both outside our homes, inside our homes and inside our purses and pockets. This heightens the requirement that we must practice our spiritual work on a daily basis, focus on God absorption and accept and sustain all awareness of Divine Love as it expresses itself to us and through us.

More Later,
Gregory

6

EGO AND SPIRITUALITY

Dear One,

Despite the claims of some that the ego must be dropped, it is an essential tool for living the spiritual life. Psychologists, sociologists and others readily recognize that the problems of the human ego contribute to the difficulties people often experience. Self-esteem, bouts of anger and even suicide are clearly linked to ego. What is seldom understood and even often misunderstood is the relationship of the ego to one's spiritual identity. How important is the ego for one's spiritual development and spiritual journey?

Some stress egolessness as a strategy for preventing the ego from interfering with or inhibiting spiritually-based actions. This is incorrect. The ego is a necessary device for managing oneself in any of the higher or lower worlds and spiritual domains. Why? Because the ego not only provides a sense of location in reference to the center from which individual action is taken, based on what is perceived, but it is the instrument and vehicle through which God wisdom manifests. The emphases made by some upon Oneness overlooks the true importance of knowing or recognizing and respectfully acknowledging one's location, both spiritually and physically. One must have the simultaneous awareness of sharing and participating in the higher consciousness. Without the perceptions of ego, one cannot distinguish between or among those actions properly his and those actions respectfully of others. This could be described as spiritually attuned judgment.

Instead of egolessness, I would propose that what is meant is ego in complete alignment with Soul, Source, God, the Creator and so on. In the Buddhist path, this might be known as Dharma, right action. Right action is the result of complete inner alignment with one's life contract, higher self, divine will and freedom from the karma of past deeds. Such is the intentional result of Sourccination designed by the higher beings to spark the Ascension of individuals into higher domains of awareness. But such cannot be maintained without diligent application of one's own spiritual disciplines.

In communications workshops that I took years ago, I learned two interesting ideas: over responsibility and under responsibility. The former is acting or taking actions that intrude upon those of others. The latter is failing to take, or simply avoiding actions that are one's own responsibility and need to be acted upon, or shifting the responsibility to someone else. The clearest example of

over responsibility is of someone doing something ostensibly on behalf of another without the other's permission or agreement. Under responsibility shows up when a person clearly has a duty to perform some action, and simply, "wimps out." Often those who believe they are living the spiritual life take the under responsible route in fear of earning karma. They do not understand that karma does not result from specific actions. Karma is created by the emotional thought energy of those actions of the doer. Any action done or performed in a neutral state of being will, by definition, be karma free.

Reactions and repercussions are simply the reality of the laws of the physical universe. For every action, there is an equal and opposite reaction. If you go out into the rain without your umbrella, you will get wet. Action: left umbrella. Reaction: wetness. If you blame, get upset or cry because you are wet, be prepared for some event to occur that gives an opportunity to experience neutrality or non-attachment under similar conditions. A bird might make a deposit on your auto. Something may be dropped. A phone message might get lost and so on. Someone may cut you off in a driving lane or take your parking space. The major lesson for us all in this universe is one of learning how to be spiritually neutral. If we learn anything else while here, it is truly a gift.

For every action, there is a reaction. This lays the groundwork for understanding ego in a spiritual context and helps explain emphases on non-attachment, God absorption and the middle path. These are not goals in themselves but simply means toward other means, i.e., techniques in preparation for accepting higher levels of consciousness. Ways of being via multiple Ascensions are themselves means toward domains of Source consciousness and freedom from even the creation of karma, which itself is a means toward living as Source, which is yet another set of means toward even other means, and so on, to and through infinity.

Gregory.

7

LIVING IN THE LIGHT

Gregory, the topic we wish to discuss is "Living in the Light." You recently received a letter from a dear friend complaining about all the darkness and despair in which he is currently living. After months of receiving such from him, you decided that you had had it and upbraided him, sternly warning him of the consequences of focusing on the negatives of his life and reminded him of the necessity of keeping his attention elsewhere. In essence, not only were you reminding him of the power of attention, you were giving him the keys to living in the light. In all your communications, you have reminded people of the necessity to receive Ascension at the hands, so to speak, of one so endowed as are the Light Givers. This is because, in order for one to enter the higher vibration, assistance is required from one so established already. To some, this experience is akin to receiving Light. Those who receive Light in this way and are able to maintain it can do so because of the many disciplines they have practiced up to that point. But the core discipline learned has been the power of personal and responsible attention, i.e., maintaining their focus on the spiritual center of all life.

The need for maintaining focus on the spiritual center has been taught in so many ways, i.e., chant the holy names of God, pray without ceasing, practicing the Presence of God and so forth. The point is quite simple, one is simply unable to sustain oneself in the Divine Consciousness without having mastered the discipline of focused attention. Now, this is not to find fault with those unable to keep their attention centered. Indeed, the whole purpose of human existence is to master the art of centered attention. Your ex-wife often scoffed at this idea. She would challenge you, "Are you telling ME that the whole purpose of life is to learn how to keep your attention centered on God?" Well, it is. At least to begin with. So, it is no surprise that for most people, the nature of being human is so distracting that, even to sit for 10-15 minutes in meditation is daunting. It just can't be done because of all the distractions, ideas and thoughts that come flooding in. But what many do not understand is that in the higher vibrations, the inability to easily and comfortably keep the attention centered forces the individual to revert to the frequencies of life where the attention is predominant. So, if the attention is mainly on darkness, distress and anguish, therein will the individual reside.

Are we being clear here? This should not be a surprise to anyone that reads this. In other words, there will be no great rescue of individuals that allow themselves to be trapped in darkness. Darkness, unfortunately, is the hole out of which one must extract himself through the practice of gently placing his attention on the spiritual center of life, be it Allah, Yahweh, Jesus, Buddha, Mahanta, ECK, Source or any of a variety of Gods, Spiritual teachers and others so endowed. Such must be done until the spark of attention transforms into raging inferno or torrent of God. More than being firmly fixed, the attention is inseparable for the true realities of God.

Others have observed that God Realization is not manifest until God is seen everywhere.

To return to the idea central to this message, the question is not really how do we live in the light, but how can we become and Be Light. First, just as we struggle to get to work every day, struggle to incorporate new ideas and ways of doing things into our lives, make every effort to make our relationships work, so must similar effort be made to live in the Light and to become light. Make no mistake, the structure and process of being human is strongly opposed to living in the Light. So, every thing in the physical, social and psychological environment acts to counteract one's focus on the spiritual center: television, sex, relationships, work and so on. There is an irony to all this. That being, when one truly understands and begins to master the art of living in Light, each area of life becomes not only simpler but transparent. one sees God or Source Is not only the architect of All that is, but It of itself is All that is. So, your advice to your dearest friend was right on target. You reminded him that his attention summons more of that upon which his attention is. So darkness begets darkness. Despair begets despair. Lack generates more lack. Rather than bemoaning one's circumstance. Rejoice because he has now the opportunity to strengthen his focus on the spiritual center of life. It is not enough to read and understand the wisdom presented and discussed by others. It is not enough to occasionally practice contemplation. It is not enough to profess an inability to stay spiritually focused. The person that wishes to Ascend and maintain the Ascended consciousness must prepare for it by recognizing, learning and practicing the disciplines of focused attention.

You ended your email to him by saying, "Quit your whining. You are a spiritual master be One." You reminded him of the biblical story of Job, who refused to take his mind off God and refused to see the tragedy of his life as anything other than God's blessings. Eventually, Job's trials and tribulations began to abate and he was restored.

We are not holding forth here that all things bad, awful and terrible will be remedied as was Job's experience. The emphasis is not on solving life's problems. The emphasis is on holding onto "God's Unchanging Hand," in the words of the spiritual. "Build Your Hopes on Things Eternal," the spiritual goes on to say.

We say the same thing to those who would enter the ranks of the Ascension Masters. Be who you are. Do the work and we will give you the even higher Ascensions when you are ready.

Hold on. You ARE a Light Being already.

Gregory

8

BEING THE GOD MAN

Dear Gregory,

In private conversations, you have described yourself as "the God Man." To some this might sound like you are being hopeful and to others, this could sound like you are bragging. What many do not understand is that there are various degrees or levels of being a 'God Man." The first level is that of the individual that spend much of his time searching for God. He reads everything he can on topics related to God. He spends countless hours discussing God and thinking about the experience of God. He may even spend years seeking the company of those that seem to have had direct experience of God. The second level of the God Man involves seeking the direct experience of God. This may come through initiations, Shakti pats, deekshas, soul travel, soul journey, out of body experiences and so. Each of these is comparable to gaining glimpses of the God experience and serve to condition the consciousness of the individual to the true, total and complete experience of God via Ascension.

The true experience of God via Ascension differs from these others in the following ways. Each occurs within the context of daily life and is tempered by the distractions, emotions and temporal illusions that accompany the human existence. They are much like the individual who wishes to know about the ocean. So he studies it from afar. He may read books written by oceanographers. Look at maps and pictures of oceans. He may even view videos and documentaries presented by adventurers and explorers. Indeed, he may look at the ocean from mountain tops, beaches and maybe even the porches of friends. He may even sip ocean water to learn its flavor, which is much like the experience of initiation. But, guess what, he has not yet waded into the ocean, felt its currents or immersed itself into its mighty depths. Only through the experience of Ascension, can one truly begin to appreciate the experience of God in all its fullness. By no means are we saying that the initial experience of Ascension will give one the total experience of God or Source, but one will gain a greater appreciation of what Ascension provides.

In all the experiences gained prior Ascension, one's experiences occur within what some call the worlds of cause and effect, the worlds of causation. So the individual, by definition, understands what is being experienced in reference to external circumstances. All occurs within the context of something else. Indeed, while it is occurring, quite often the thoughts are on something else. Consider the following examples:

1. What's being said here is so different from…
2. I wonder if MY initiation experience is the same as or different from…
3. I wonder if I'm ready for MY next…
4. Am I at the same level or higher than…
5. Wow! That felt wonderful when it happened but now…
6. When will I see the Master again…
7. Wow! They are so lucky to be with the Master…

Please do not misunderstand, we are not belittling any of these experiences. All are necessary on the path to God or Source consciousness. But they are not substitutes for God consciousness and many mistake these temporary stopping points as the true experience of God. If the ocean is our metaphor, these are comparable to tide pools, nothing but puddles populated with aspects representative of God, but, in no way comparable to the unfathomable depths of Ascension.

So, what makes Ascension so different. The answer is quite simple. There are no references in the experience of Ascension to anything other than Source. In the Ascended state, you are truly without a context. You are without reference to others in any way. Your experience is your own. You are outside the worlds of causation and effects. However, initially, your mind, which is not only unfamiliar with the content and experience of Soul Ascension, will struggle mightily to make sense of this new experience. In fact, it will try to translate and define what is going on. This must be ignored. How do you do this? Simply tell the mind, which is an intelligent being, "Be still, I love you, let ME experience this directly without any help from you." It will follow your instructions. By so doing, it and you enter into the fullness of Soul Ascension.

We are distinguishing here between Soul Ascension and higher levels, such as God Ascension, Source Ascension and others. Now, why is Soul Ascension important? It is because, for most, in this time, it is the first time they have the opportunity not only to experience themselves unbounded and but also able to maintain themselves in that state. The latter point is crucial to understanding what the true gift of the Light Giver program, i.e. to support the expansion of individual consciousness outside the worlds of cause and effect. This re-establishes the individual's attention not only to a wider focus, but also recenters it on Godhood. Most importantly, individual responsibility and freedom to choose even higher states of Beingness are affirmed. And here the journey truly begins.

We began by discussing the idea of "the God Man." This is the being that the Ascension Master must become, the individual that is so centered in the experience of God that despite all visible failings and failures, he and we know that God moves and has Its being fully in his consciousness. When the body stops, when the mind stops, when all is gone, only God remains; only he remains

This is the God man, who you are and who the Ascension Masters must become. Even yet, there are higher levels: These we know as Ascended Masters, Archangels, Time Lords, Sugmads, Gods, Silent Ones, Immortals, and so on.

Do not tarry on the path. Master the spiritual consciousness. Ascension is yours. Seize it!

Gregory

THE ART OF SURRENDER

Dear Gregory,

In this message we revisit a familiar topic, the art of surrender. This topic important because it receives so much attention in many of the spiritual teachings. Some have been told surrender to the Master, surrender to God, surrender to Spirit, even surrender yourself and so on. As an extension to that, many connect the concept of detachment and non attachment to notion of surrender. The problem with each of these ideas is that they are taught and considered in relationship to something else such as the Master, Spirit, God and yourself. Indeed in order to be detached, or non attached, there is embedded the idea that there is something from which one is either detached or not attached. What many actually get from such ideas is the importance of either the thing one to which one is surrendering or the thing from which one is detached or non-attached. The nature of living in the dual worlds is life in a world of opposites.

So, if by definition, surrender includes opposite elements, then true surrender cannot occur because both elements are present.

Examples of duality: black-white, up-down, yes-no and so forth. So, to sharpen the point, if we say there is black, white is implied. If we say up, down is implied and present in the concept whether or not it is said aloud. If one thinks "detachment," the thing from which I wish to be detached is implied. What we are pointing out to you is that the typical reference to surrender is embedded with an implied concept of non-surrender because a thing is embedded within the very idea.

It is not like the individual who, caught in a swamp grasps a vine hopefully to pull himself out of the muck, only to discover the vine originates in the same swamp in which he is trapped. As hopeful as he may be, the harder he grasps the vine, the more embedded he is in the muck. So much for surrendering to anything.

The emphasis in the Ascension work is consistently on the experience of it.

Those who accept Soul Ascension are cautioned to ignore all efforts of the mind to define, understand, make sense of, interpret, judge or evaluate in any way the Ascension experience. This, of course, is difficult for most, because the human generally depends on the mind to make sense of one's external world. How the experience of Ascension confuses the mind with is that the mind requires reference points and measures. There are simply no reference points within the experience of Ascension, except God. The mind simply cannot measure the experience of Ascension. Ascension occurs in domains inaccessible to the mind, except as enlightenment. We discuss the enlightenment in another message. But for now, let it be understood that enlightenment bypasses directly mental activities to see and understand at the Soul level, make clear the nature of reality and experience. Enlightenment is not a thinking activity;it relies on seeing, realizing and being. For example, Gregory is somewhat enlightened, which makes it easier for us to use his services to put these ideas into English. We do not speak English. Nor, for that matter do we speak any human language from where we are located in the cosmos. But just as your nervous impulses are translated into body movement, so are our thought impulses translated telepathically into the words you now read.

We do wish to clarify the point about Gregory's enlightenment. At moments like this and even when questioned about spirituality, spiritual truths and such, Gregory easily shifts into an enlightened state of awareness that is available to those in Ascension, like you are or will be. As an enlightened being, there are degrees of contact that one may have with not only Source of itself, but also to spiritual wisdom only accessible via enlightenment.

In such a state, it is like a cosmic spiritual Google. So, when a topic is suggested by us intuitively to Gregory, the channel opens up and our wisdom floods his consciousness. This is at least that to which you may aspire as an Ascension Master. Human beings are linked to and experience such wisdom in varying degrees. For some it is via intuition, an inner voice, a sense of knowing, clairvoyance and so on. Gregory, gets these dictations easily and directly.The emphasis here is not on what Gregory has achieved. This is because, in truth, Gregory has achieved nothing on his own. He was completely satisfied with aspiring to deliver workshops, Sunday sermons and talks at seminars for the rest of his life until we plucked him from that tedium. Via the individual that he accepted as his spiritual teacher at the time, Gregory was given number of life-changing Ascension experiences from a variety of higher beings. These included various robes, Archangels, Time Lords, deities, Silent Ones others still unnamed. A job needed to be done; Gregory was at hand, so he will given this assignment.

Nevetheless, Gregory's fulfillment of his mission has taken longer than we expected (and we expected it to take quite awhile) for him to fully grasp the significance of, and to undertake his charge. Under no circumstances do we seek glorification of ourselves, Gregory or this work. Our purpose is to point out that your spiritual aspirations can be easily and fully reached through the use of the spiritual tools you are being provided via Ascension.

When your focus is no longer within the worlds of duality, reference points are dropped. Your emphasis of necessity must be on the experience of Ascension. Your attention moves from outward attention and mental attention, to the experience of surrender, which has no reference point other than the experience of it.

If it were compared to leaping off a cliff, the truly surrendered individual thinks neither of the cliff he left or the rocks below. His awareness is solely on the experience of the leap and knowing that the leap is into a new state of consciousness. He is not falling; he is transforming. He is not surrendering. He is surrendered and that is his new and permanent state of consciousness. So what do you surrender to?

Note the following:

You surrender to no-thing.
You surrender to.
You surrender.
You.

10

YOU ARE LOVE

Dear Gregory,

In this message, we discuss the essential nature of the act of love as a necessary but insufficient condition for the Ascension Master. Down through the ages, in various discourse, parables and lessons, we are reminded that acts of love are essential to living the spiritual life. So many people, believing they have captured the essence of what is meant by love, spend their lives engaged in acts of love. What they fail to understand that love is not an act; it is not something that is done to or for another. Love is a way of being in the world. If such manifests, then every action can be an act of love, whether or not its consequences result in happy circumstances. To repeat, Love is a way of Being in such a way that every action is, in fact, an act of love.

Our aim here is not to minimize acts of love. They are important and are, indeed, necessary steps in the direction of becoming a completely loving being. The disciplines that must be practiced to reach the pure loving state are beyond the imagination of most people. Why? Because the disciplines require require the reconditioning of the mind in response to all thoughts and actions. Victor Frankl, a world famous psychiatrist, was able to stay alive in a Nazi concentration camp by choosing to be joyful rather than depressed. It is clear that everything we see, hear and think stimulates a response of some type. Thus, we propose that if you are serious about being a loving, God-filled being, spend time associating love with every thing that enters your awareness. We are not proposing that you tell your shopping basket how much you love it while in the supermarket or that you discourse with each item in the frozen food section, but, mentally, you can certainly think some "I love yous" to everything and everybody you see.

Even as you read this, feel free to send us some loving thoughts to us, your computer, the monitor screen, the paper on which these words are printed, your desk. Let everything upon which your glance falls feel the love. Try walking through a hall in your home; send love to everything you see. Notice the feelings of love that are returned. We suggest that you not openly discuss this practice with others until it has become a part of your way of being. We guarantee that, once it has become a part of who you are, you will find it unnecessary to discuss eventhe topic of love with others.

Let everything you do, even the things that you didn't like to do, be an act of love. Try not to personalize this feeling of love. If that need is felt, personalize the feeling to the God of your understanding orto Source. Under no circumstances, should you pepper your loved ones with "I love yous" to a level beyond what they experienced before you undertook this practice.

What you will begin to see, as time passes, that many of the "divine" virtues manifest simply and naturally. These include humility, kindness, mercy, forgiveness, etc. Filled with love, there's no need to "work on oneself" and there's no need to make efforts toward consistency, Sometimes you will donate. Others times not. Sometimes you will hold doors open; sometimes not. But you will be mostly be kind, considerate and gentle. But not always. And, sometimes, you may not be loving.

After all, you are human. Inconsistency goes with the territory.

There is an irony in all this. Many lightworkers spend as much time as possible in transformative silent retreats where inner practices of love are emphasized. If the emphases are not maintained afterward, the learning is lost and any experienced transformation is lost. Remember, Love is not something you do. Better to be silent and filled with love in the hubbub of daily life until you fully experience and realize that Love is truly who you are.

Don't be in love. Let love be in you.
Be Love.
Just Be.

11

THE ART OF ENLIGHTENMENT

Dear Gregory,

In this message, we extend our discussion of enlightenment, a topic that has been given quite a bit of attention down through the ages. Yet of many spiritual concepts, it may be the most poorly understood. Why? Because of spiritual concepts that abound, such as humility, honor, love, kindness and so on, enlightenment is the most comprehensive and inclusive spiritual concent.

Many see enlightenment as occurring after one has spent decades diligently applying oneself to all manner of spiritual practices. Yet most think reserved to that are truly blessed by God and his holy angels. Moments of enlightenment are often overridden by fears, doubts and external circumstances. But, in a fleeting moment, enlightment may occur.

The truth of the matter is that enlightenment is is wholistic, in that it takes into account not only spiritual insight, but also an awareness of the implications for spiritual action. One cannot be fully enlightened without understanding in the moment how the insight translates directly into life experience. Enlightenment via Ascension, most importantly, brings with it the awareness of the spiritual freedom of others and their right, indeed their responsibility to guide their actions by their own sources of wisdom and understanding. An individual that wishes to use his "enlightenment" to direct or override the wishes of others is in the grips of something that might only be called an enlightenment illusion.

So, what is enlightenment, really. It is the full immersion of one's awareness into what can best be described as the God mind. In that state, one is no longer trapped in the worlds of duality, the worlds of cause and effect, the world of Maya and illusion. Instead, one is in the timeless dimension of the immortal consciousness and sees or senses, within one's own field of awareness, limitless possibilities, infinite awareness and the totality of life. The importance of one's own thought diminishes. The significance of one's own words pales before the significance of others' humanity. The awareness of life is interpenetrated with a peace and love that "passes all understanding."

We are not proposing that, when you enter enlightenment, you should trade in your suits, dresses and other modern outerware for saffron roles. You could. No. What we do propose is that you spend the appropriate amount of time in your spiritual practice, that you eschew strong emotion, and that you cherish and extend the moments of enlightenment that are yours. Be assured that, as the Ascension Master, there will be greater moments of enlightenment, whether they result from your spiritual disciplines, or blessings given by us or Gregory, but there will be greater moments of enlightenment. These you must treasure because they are gifts from your higher self and represent, even more so that you are moving more deeply into the consciousness of the Ascension Master. The God Mind is yours. As you do this work, there will be a gradual expansion of the channel between your Soul Awareness and your God Awareness via the higher Self. Eventually, your higher self and your Soul Awareness will fully integrate. In that instance, a steady state of enlightenment will manifest. Then, you will

Be Still and Know.
Such is the essence of enlightenment.
Gregory

12

THE LIGHTGIVERS, NOT A SPIRITUAL PATH

In this, the final message in this series, we will explain why the Light Giver Program is not a spiritual path.

To reach this point, you have most likely participated in more than one spiritual path or religion. You may also have experienced as a client or as a practitioner a number of healing modalities. Gregory, for example, began his religious practice as the son of a Baptist fundamentalist minister. He migrated through atheism, Unitarianism, and at least two or three spiritual paths. Today he is dividing his services between the Light Giver program and groups that practice the direct experience of God.

Like Gregory, your search may have been to better understand that known as God and, quite possibly, healings. The question that underlies each of these is reflected on Gregory's wife's refusal to believe that the purpose of life is to learn how to be continuously present in God. Another way of saying it would be to realize that God is continuously present in one's life and that any other perception of life is illusionary. This does not mean that life's realities must be ignored. It only means that life's realities are of lesser importance than the reality of God.

To help clarify this point, let's unbundle what are spiritual paths and religions. In almost every instance, each claims to contain the spiritual truths that are necessary and sufficient to reach God. Few, if any claim to teach what it takes to become fully and completely integrated with God or Source. Yet almost all religions and spiritual paths revere individuals that have become such. But, in almost no case have these individuals sketched the architecture of their path to the God head, the aery details of the process by which their personal divinity was achieved. Spiritual paths and religions are most often overlaid with books, writings, discourses and other materials that offer ideas, concepts and principles propounded by their founders. Brief mention is made of contacts or visits with some great spiritual being that transmitted the higher consciousness. We know, as Light Givers, that nothing was truly transmitted. In fact, the guru, Ascended Master, Archangel or other higher being simply adjusted the individual's vibration to allow a higher consciousness to manifest.

In the meantime, followers are lead to believe that by reading, reviewing, contemplating and remembering all the words of wisdom, a higher state of awareness might be achieved. Nothing could be farther from the truth. Given the plethora of materials available, it is much more likely that the only thing that can be assured is a headache. Even at the highest level, no spiritual path can lead to God or Source. What the path may best do is lead one to the representation of God upon which the path has focused. For this reason, some say, behind the face of God is God itself. But to enter that reality, the assistance of higher beings is required. This is the law.

All this means is that once one reaches the highest level of the path, the journey or realization of God itself truly begins. The support of one that has made the journey is required.

There are two reasons why individuals do not go beyond the highest levels of their religion or path. The first is that they are trapped within their respective organizations. Organizations have a primary purpose, that is, to ensure their own survival, which may or may not include the actual survival of what the founder taught and not necessarily meeting the spiritual aims of their adherents. This, of course, includes both spiritual organizations and spiritual hierarchies.

The second reason is that quite often, neither the founder, teacher nor the organization's leaders may have the wisdom or other tools like Ascension to assist their followers, no matter how motivated they may be. Simply stated the follower or seeker may have simply gone as far as they can go in their religion or spiritual path.

For this reason, you must understand that the purpose of the Light Giver Ascension program is to support those that have reached the heights of their spiritual pursuits with Sourccination. By so doing, all spiritual blockages are removed at the Auric and Soul levels and Ascension is experienced. Thus, individuals enter the respective spiritual realm to which they aspire: Nirvana Sartori, Jivan Mukti, the void, Eckshar, Soul Domain the Kingdom of Heaven and so on. Central to this work is the focus on Source of itself, which is understood to be beyond the God Consciousness experience. That involves the clearing and replacing with Divine energy of all vestiges and remnants of the worlds of cause and effect.

With the completion of God Ascension, the opportunity for Source Ascension is present, which begins the true absorption and migration into Source Consciousness.

GOLDEN AGE LIGHT GIVER MESSAGES

1 - 12

GOLDEN AGE LIGHT GIVER MESSAGE 1

—⟋𝓂⟍—

In this message we emphasize the purpose of the spiritual life and the essential nature of spiritual exercises. In the next, we will explain why these are the "Golden Age" Light Giver Messages.

We are the Light Givers. Gregory, we are delighted that you are so directly accessible to us without all the preparations required by other instruments. Your channel is wide open and that you may type our thoughts directly is wonderful, as you might say, in human talk.

Today, we wish to discuss the purpose of life on earth. There are many who are so enmeshed in the illusions and distortions of life that they fail to recognize its true purpose, that being that which has been discussed and presented by holy men, MY stics, savants, spiritual guides and messengers down through the ages. Stated quite simply, the purpose of life is to return to the God or Source state. There is no other reason for life on earth or anywhere. The Creator has replicated itself or himself, if one wishes to think anthropomorphically (this includes herself, too, for those with a feminist bent), in billions of forms or cells, you might say. And in so doing, this has allowed the creation of various distortions and illusions in which the cells, in this case we humans, have found ourselves. The essential purpose of such experience is to strengthen the individual intention of spiritual survival, which when accomplished, brings back to the creator certain restorative energies that, in turn, perpetuate its own eternal existence.

Thus, life on earth is not only critical to each of us on the planet, wherever we are, but it is critical and essential for the continuity and maintenance of life throughout the universe. There are some who would characterize this as some sort of cosmic game, who would see it as nothing but some sort of Divine charade. Such is not the case; it is an essential and perpetual inevitable journey through time and space that each unit of consciousness must go through, resulting eventually in complete merger with the Divine Source of all wisdom. There are no exceptions and no excuses.

So, the question that one must face is how one may continue within the Divine illusion and accomplish, in all truth, one's spiritual goals. For this reason, spiritual practices such as prayer, meditation, chanting, yoga, tai chi, even walking and running meditations are essential. Why? Because the instrument or body that we have has essentially two attunements. One is a very strong and positive attunement to the world of senses and sensations and is designed for the survival of the physical body and its accoutrements, such as emotions, memories, conscious and subconscious thoughts. These are all given so that the human may persist long enough in the respective incarnation to accomplish those spiritual goals that have been accepted for that incarnation. The second is a very strong and positive attunement to the inner world of spirit and Source. Therein lays the dialectic of human consciousness and the power of choice, in that the human must find balance between both these twin impulses. One is to be completely immersed, if not overwhelmed, by the strength of environmental influences. The other is to be completely absorbed by and absorbed into the inner worlds of Source. Clearly, there are certain risks to both.

The complete absorption into the external world of sensation submits the individual's action and life to one of impulses and reactions, much like a bouncing ball, without direction. On the other hand, the complete absorption into the inner world obviates whatever responsibility the individual might have to others, related for love, service and duty. So, the challenge to the one on the path of accomplishing spiritual goals is how to find whatever can or must be done to fully invest in each.

There is in some spiritual paths a strong reliance on prayer, meditation, contemplation and the other spiritual practices that we have mentioned. What many don't fully realize is that these each are not ends in themselves. In fact, while one might say they are means to an end, the fact of the matter is that they are means to other means, that are themselves means to other means, and so on. While it is generally agreed that we are One and that emphasis should be placed on our Oneness, there is a seldom noticed separation between this goal and the spiritual practices in which people are engaged. For example, in some spiritual practices, there is an emphasis of putting one's attention upon a spiritual center, quite often the Tisral Til or Third Eye, that overlaps the pineal gland. While this is truly necessary, it is not the ultimate purpose of such an exercise. The ultimate purpose is to broaden one's perspective beyond the screen of the mind that appears in such a way that the contemplator's awareness expands in multiple ways. Clearly, the way in which it expands will depend upon the channels or avenues for one's spiritual growth. There could be greater wisdom, views of distant vistas, past lives, deeper intuitions, or out of body experiences that reinforce one's own immortality, conscious contact with other sentient beings, and so on.

All that notwithstanding, the immersion via the spiritual exercise in Source has the essential purpose of shifting the focus of the individual's life, so that there is not life out here or just life in there, but that there is but one life, lived fully in Source, that enshrouds all that is said and done. Of course, there will be moments when this cannot be fully adhered to, but, in the main, the spiritual life to which one aspires must encapsulate every single aspect.

So, how does this occur? Again, the spiritual teachers have shared the means, such as being able to keep the attention on a spiritual point, such as God. We counsel against putting the attention on a person or personality, although this is a good temporary tool, if only for the benefit of the practice. (Gregory, we do enjoy our rapport with your thinking process. How truly delightful.) So, chanting the names of God, one's initiatory word, seeing God in others, practicing the outflow of love, are all worthy techniques, etc. We also strongly recommend the blessing practice that Gregory brought over from the Universal Healer program. This is the idea of sending blessing energy on your own, as frequently as possible throughout the day, to Source, friends, family, enemies, projects, activities, even to the person who just cut you off on the freeway or took your parking space. The thrust of such work is to assure your permanence in the heaven worlds through your absorption and expression of Source energies.

It is no contradiction to say that, if one wishes to be One with God, one must be single-minded on that topic. It must be like the air we breathe, the music we hear, the beat of our hearts, the drum of our heels upon the pavement and even the raindrops falling from the sky. Let us leave off here. We will pick this up later.

Gregory, with you as our transmitting vehicle, we install within this message, sufficient energy to unlock the hearing and seeing of those with whom you share these words, the wisdom contained within, if they are so willing.

The Light Givers

GOLDEN AGE LIGHT GIVER MESSAGE 2

—⁓𝕸⁓—

Gregory: I am ready.

The Light Givers: We are the Light Givers. In this session, we will clarify why we have agreed to call these messages, "Golden Age." There is a debate among those who have focused their scholarship on the year 2012. The focus, however, is one of good reason. It has been duly noted that many of the ancient calendars end at 2012 signaling the end of something, and quite likely the beginning of something else. On the one hand, there are those who believe that the world will end somewhat like the end depicted in the film, *2012*, in which there are cataclysms such as earthquakes and tsunamis that culminated in a huge flood. The predictions of disasters are based on scientific evidence related to geographic and tectonic changes resulting from shifts in the earth's axis, due to long-term wobbles in its rotation, called precession. Research now indicates that this wobble climaxes in a complete polar shift every 26,000 years, thereby resulting in the destruction of ancient civilizations and the loss of life on an unbelievable scale.

On the other hand, there are those who believe that, while some level of disasters might occur, a Golden Age will ensue with a transformation in human consciousness, completing an evolution to an almost divine state of being. Not only is the year 2012 a fixture in the ancient calendars, it is even inscribed on the uppermost row of the pyramid on the US dollar bill. Even the founding fathers gave significance to 2012. If cataclysms greater than the normal state of disaster are to occur, it is beyond our ken to describe a scenario that might assure the continuity of life as you know it. We wish to assure you that a transformation in human consciousness is already underway and it is our desire and intention to do whatever we can to hasten it. Thus, we choose to call this set of messages, "Golden Age."

It is well documented that the earth, the solar system and the Milky Way galaxy in which they are embedded are moving into alignment and that the energy of that alignment concentrates cosmic forces in ways that were experienced by ancient civilizations and which have been likewise foretold by ancient prophecies. These energies magnify and accelerate our biological and spiritual evolution making predictions of heightened divinity even more possible. The emphasis is on the word "possible." While the increased energies are, in a sense, predestined, nothing can take away your freedom of choice.

We eschew the task of being alarmist and would say, whichever tack is taken, there are grounds for accelerating one's immersion in the spiritual way, in deepening one's contact with Divinity, in taking on, even more so, the holy practices, and achieving one's spiritual goals. In a very real sense, the time has come and is coming for the people of earth to take even more seriously their spiritual purpose and to acknowledge their role in the Divine plan. No matter what the scale of disaster, there will be a harvesting of Souls that have, while on earth, mastered the art of living in a higher state of consciousness that some might call being able to be karma free. By that we mean that they have lost the intention of living reactively and are completely comfortable with living lives of love and compassion. We will say that they live in the fourth dimension rather than the third dimension of strong emotions and great attachment. Those living such lives are the precursors of the Golden Age.

The Light Givers

GOLDEN AGE LIGHT GIVER MESSAGE 3

—ᗰᗰ—

The Light Givers: We are the Light Givers: Gregory, you and we must learn how to do this work together. In our haste to get you to record our thoughts despite your daily plans and activities, we gave you advance snippets that your mind began to reorganize along its own preferences, thereby resulting in this third attempt to get our thoughts accurately recorded, without distortion. In the future, please come directly to the typing instrument from either sleep or your meditation. Do nothing in between. Whatever you do will activate the mind, thereby interfering with our direct communication. Do you understand?

Gregory: Yes. I am ready. What wisdom do you wish to share today?

The Light Givers: Please begin these dictations without delay in this manner. In this session, we explore the topic of 2012 and the Golden Age. Perhaps this will explain why we title this series, "The Golden Age Messages."

The Light Givers: Today, we speak of the year 2012 and the coming so-called Golden Age. There are those who romanticize about the year 2012 and visualize extraterrestrials coming to the aid of humans to rescue them as the planet experiences cataclysmic destruction. Or, alternatively humans being transformed magically into intergalactic inter-dimensional beings, while still walking the earth, only to be whisked into higher existences. While there may be some extraterrestrial involvement, and some whisking away, in truth, the Golden Age is now. The opportunity to take on Divine attributes and to enter, in consciousness, the Golden Age via Ascension has never been more available in this cycle.

In truth, the Golden Age experience is the Ascension into higher consciousness of those that have taken the time to reach the heights of their spiritual aspirations. What could be more golden than the removal of all spiritual blockages, complete alignment with your spiritual purpose, and the elimination of your karma, and with higher Ascensions, the elimination of even the power to create karma? This is the program of activity that we have given to the Light Givers still in human embodiment. Why cling to old forms, teachers, philosophers and masters that do not release you into the golden consciousness that you have earned and truly deserve? The message of 2012 is that without entering the fourth dimensional consciousness, one has no choice but to continue the reincarnation cycle of the third dimension.

The history of this planet is replete with evidence that the cycle of disaster foretold or implied by the 2012 calendars has come many times. Why? Because this planet, this speck of cosmic dust repeats a journey throughout the universe over and over again. And each time that it travels this path it goes through a predictable cycle. How is it that the ancient Sumerians and many others have in their records information about the entire universe and even galaxies and stars only recently apparent to modern scientists and astronomers via the Hubble telescope? How is it that ancient civilizations, such as those in Egypt, were able to construct monuments like the pyramids that today cannot be duplicated? Even the American Founding fathers knew that 2012 was significant, embedding it at the top line of the pyramid under the third eye on the dollar bill. The significance of 2012 cannot simply be ignored in the hope that the year will come and go.

Mankind has raised to great heights many times, somewhat like the great king, Sisyphus, who was doomed to roll a boulder up a hill, only to have it slip from his grasp once he neared the top, then to repeat his climb again and again. The Golden Age where mankind become as gods and walk the earth with great spiritual powers is not entirely a foolish dream. The time for mankind to walk the earth as gods is now.

This, then, is the true Golden Age. This civilization has reached its heights. Its occupants must either be Ascended, at least into the fourth dimensional reality, or remain in the third dimension of reincarnation. Do this out of love for Source, God, your higher self and all life. Have no fear. Welcome to the Golden Age. Any rescues to be done will be of your own creation via meditation, contemplation or any of the many spiritual tools and disciplines that lead to the Ascension of consciousness. (Gregory, we note your edits. They are acceptable to us. Thank you.)

The Light Givers: This ends this session.
Gregory: Thank you.

GOLDEN AGE LIGHT GIVER MESSAGE 4

———〰〰〰———

We are the Light Givers: Today we wish to speak of the eternal life which you call immortality. What is not clear to many is that the natural state of being is eternal instead of temporary as is experienced in the human state of existence. Think of it. There are sayings in your world such as, "Everybody dies," "No one lives forever," "You can't take it with you," referring to wealth, and so on.

The reality is that the natural state of existence is to live forever. It is an aberration of life to live only temporarily. The temporary condition that you experience is simply a function of taking on coverings that by definition have a limited existence. Think of it, the natural state of being is one of eternality. In addition, there is also the viewpoint that emotions such as anger, hate, fear and so on are natural. Thus, the statement, "He is only human, what do you expect?" Again, the natural state of being does not include such aberrations or distortions. In the natural state, one lives in a continuous condition of love, gratitude and joy. The distortions that you experience such as emotions, fear, sense of loss, etc., are, strictly speaking, unnatural. So, the entire human existence is devoted to learning how to divest oneself of such distortions and of returning to one's natural state of being while embedded in a sea of such distortions.

How can this transition be made? Actually, it's quite easy. All the spiritual works are replete with systems designed to escape living the distorted life apart from one's natural state, but many people allow themselves to become soaked with the essence of the distortions and come to believe that their natural state of being is one sodden with the essence of the distortions. They live out the fantasies induced by the energies of the worlds in which they find themselves. How sad, to characterize such in a human fashion, when the true reality is as close as one's fingertips. For this reason, many paths speak of not living in maya or illusion, pointing out that the phenomena of life are not the true reality.

Let us return once again to the image of living the eternal life. Just think of it for a moment. Imagine yourself as an eternal being. Know in this moment that you really do exist forever, that immortality is not something to which you aspire. Indeed, it is something that you are. What is it now that interferes, if at all, with that image? In many cases, there is a sense of finiteness, a sense of incompleteness, a sense of temporariness that overwhelms one's imagination. How, in the face, of seeing the deaths of others, of seeing the horrors of war, of famine, of disease, and so on, could one possibly believe in immortality? Therein lays the problem "Believe." Believing is simply a mental activity, a configuring of thoughts and ideas, undergirded by hopeful expectation. Immortality is one of knowing or being, one of isness-ness. Belief only occurs within the finite worlds. The sense of immortality occurs solely within the infinite world.

Until one's own quantum force is freed from spiritual blockages that may include self-imposed limitations, one remains stuck in a world of unfettered emotions and limitations. Until one becomes completely aligned with their spiritual purpose, they are forced to remain less spiritual achievers, and more spiritual wanderers. Until one has experienced true Ascension they remain dependent upon the thoughts and ideas of others for spiritual understanding and hopeful that they, too, will be graced with spiritual wisdom. For these reasons, we have established the Light Giver program of healings, clearings and Ascension. Once the blinders of spiritual blockages have been dropped and your alignment with Soul purpose, along with the elimination of karma, has occurred, the gift of Ascension is given. In that state of Being, one experiences the infinity consciousness, eternal love and gratitude, and the immortal consciousness.

We acknowledge that throughout life, people are given glimpses of immortality: gratitude, love, knowingness, timelessness, and so on. These are the gifts of the creator that give you a sense of what awaits you, when you move outside the veil of the mortal existence when you leave the worlds of time, space and matter; when you establish yourself above the mountains of humanity; when you enter the folds of the Creator and accept and live as the immortal Being that you truly are. But, even then, as long as you are embodied, you must enter via meditation or some other spiritual practice, the immortal consciousness of the Creator often and regularly, until you are no longer hidden within the physical body.

The Light Givers

GOLDEN AGE LIGHT GIVER MESSAGE 5

—⁓ℳ⁓—

We are the Light Givers: Today, we wish to speak of bringing the physical body into harmony with the desires of the Creator for it and its external environmental challenges, i.e. physical health. A few years ago, several writers predicted that human desires were being manipulated with scientists, ad men, and others for the purpose of profits earned from the sale of various materials, such as food, clothes, cars, etc. It was their contention that studies would be made of the tastes and preferences of the general public and that ad campaigns would be undertaken to capitalize on the public's unconscious vulnerabilities. These included books by Vance Packard and by John Kenneth Galbraith; Packard's book was *The Hidden Persuaders* and Galbraith's was *The New Industrial State*. Both noted the enormous effects that could manipulate people's buying habits and tastes. So, buying habits are a result of unconscious manipulations.

Elsewhere, we note the role of the body covering in obscuring one's own sense of immortality. But it is a role exacerbated by the substances and energies in which the body covering, its organs, glands, and cells, are bathed. These include vegetables that are drenched with various poisonous substances, the carcasses of birds, fish, and animals that are filled with various chemicals and liquids for both internal and external use that are combinations of unhealthy chemicals, whether carbonated drinks or lotions and dyes for external use. What is not apparent to users is that such chemicals taken internally or used externally not only pollute the body covering, but they interfere with the physical function of the body resulting quite often in health problems.

In addition to all this, people are deluged with deadly energies continuously. Millions of cell phones, GPS devices, microwaves, satellite transmissions, radio and television signals, electric cables and so on, bombard each of you constantly. In addition to living in completely polluted physical vehicles, you are awash in a sea of energy pollution that directly interferes with the ebb and flow of energy throughout your bodies.

What can be done? There is little to be done in regard to resisting the cosmic energies around you, although some have developed protective devices for personal and home use. The effectiveness of these varies by manufacturer and must be individually investigated. The effects of the chemical poisons and foods are offset by better food choices and the use of supplements or food substitutions. For this reason, the selection and use of organic foods, however expensive it is, are wise indeed as is the reduction in the quantity and type of foods consumed. If one is immortal, it might be asked, why bother with being protected from the energy environment and with food choices. Should one not just let life run its course and exit when the times come? Certainly, but the question is what the course of one's life is.

Earlier, we mentioned the importance of survival intention as essential to spiritual development. First, each incarnation is seeded with opportunity choices that must be made in line with one's own spiritual purpose. One's own spiritual goals are aligned fully and completely with one's reincarnation cycle. To assure the accomplishment of spiritual goals, whatever steps necessary to perpetuate one's existence by limiting the poisoning of the body and it's being overwhelmed by human generated energy must be done. But it must be done, not out of fear, but out of the commitment to fulfill one's own spiritual destiny: that of achieving the immortal consciousness while still in the physical body.

To be sure, there is the strong need to free oneself of strict dependence for protein from the carcasses of dead animals and to protect oneself from the chemicals on and in food and drink. Just as it is important, if possible, to be protected from manmade energies, there is just as strong a need to be protected from the intrusive energies of others. For this reason, in addition to the removal of spiritual blockages, the Light Giver system of clearings and healings includes several steps to remove intrusive energies: cancelling prior agreements, disconnecting any negative energy from others, living or discarnate, and eliminating negative influences from the past, along with the establishment of protective energy shields. Performed in concert with one's overall life purpose, integration with the energy of the Creator and with Ascension via one's spiritual practices, the immortal consciousness can be entered and maintained while still in the physical body, thereby well preparing one for the fourth dimensional consciousness augured by 2012.

The Light Givers

GOLDEN AGE LIGHT GIVER MESSAGE 6

―――∽ɱ∽―――

Gregory: What wisdom do you have for ME today?

We are the Light Givers: Today we will speak of the grand illusion and great truth called love. Love is a term that embeds itself in rhapsodies of romance, sacrifice, charity and so forth. What is simply not understood is that the versions or visions of love had by most humans are only the barest essence of what the love energy truly is. The current concepts only hint at the barest idea of what the energy truly represents. In a sense, the love that you know is but the lowest aspect of total union with the Creator. The love that is experienced by most humans winds up being a distraction from the true manifestation of love in its highest form. Imagine if you will the magnetism of iron filings felt from a magnet, or the energy that holds the neutrons, protons and quarks of the atoms in place. Think of gravity. Would you call them love? Would you say the protons and neutrons are in love with each other? Of course not.

Interestingly enough, it is exactly the same force that you know, in the human form, as love. It is energy of Source, the most powerful attraction and binding force in the universe. In its highest form, love binds the replicas of the Creator, which are you, to the Creator. Only the illusions and distortions of the third dimensional reality prevent total union. So that every single thought, every single action, every single vision, everything is a pure reflection of the Creator. Do you see how erroneous it is to walk around everyday thinking that because you feel love for all life that somehow you are experiencing the highest form of its expression? Can you understand, therefore, how wrongly the romantic novels, books and movies limit the expression of love: to kissing, holding hands, sexual unions and looking at each other all googly eyed.

Please do not misunderstand us. There is a hint of love in those experiences, but just the barest hint. It is the difference between catching simply an aroma of perfume and being completely immersed in a vat of it. Even then, the experience of the highest form of love is even stronger than that. It would be, using this example, one in which the vat of perfume in which one is immersed soaks the individual all the way down to the atom level. But, in this case, not only would one be soaked to the atom level, but it would interpenetrate even to the quantum level and complete a merger of 100 percent, in essence becoming the perfume itself, indistinguishable from that within the vat. Of course, as long as one is in the human embodiment, it is unlikely that he or she will achieve full merger with the Creator, given all of the distractions and intrusions that occur in this vibration.

The point of this message is not to disparage the forms of love that do appear, but to discourage the oversimplification of the love energy and to shift one's attention to the purpose and highest expression of love, that being achieving total union with the Creator. It is true that if one is basically unloving, union with God will not occur. Why? A loving inclination is toward the affinity of the Creator. Of course, there is the well known catch phrase that "God is love." Likewise, there is a similar idea that "we exist because God loves us." Both of these are silly when you consider them. The Creator is much more than love; in fact, the Creator is completely outside the bounds of human thought and experience. We exist because we are God in limited manifestation with the Divine purpose of gaining unlimited manifestation.

We do not exist, in fact, because God loves us. We exist because God Is and we are a part of God. Love, as such, is merely a reflection of The Creator's affinity for itself and we exist in manifested expression. So, the experience of being human and uttering such romanticisms as "I love You" are merely hints of the union that is to come, union with God, which is far more intense and absorbing that any expression of love in the human form might find itself. Of course, we do love you and will unite with you as the Creator has united with us.

Please understand that the thrust of this message is not to disparage love, but to expand your horizon and understanding of it. It serves the purpose of opening your heart and Beingness to its expression. However, do not limit your concept of it simply to how it is experienced in the human form. Know that what you can experience is merely the barest hint of what you will experience once you are fully united with the Creator, and for this reason, it is an essential element of the human experience, one that mirrors only to a very limited extent, how you will know it, ultimately.

The Light Givers

GOLDEN AGE LIGHT GIVER MESSAGE 7

—⚶—

We are the Light Givers. Today we will speak of emotions and their purpose. For many the existence of emotions is a natural fact. This means they expect to respond to life's issues and circumstances emotionally. They accept the fact that everything that occurs around them and to them will result in emotions. Likewise, they are seldom surprised when others react similarly. But what is unexamined is why humans are vested with emotions. What roles do emotions play in life, and even more specifically, how are they related to the spiritual journeys on which we all are?

The fact is, as we can imagine, emotions are nothing but energy expressions. But what is the basis and purpose of emotions. There are two purposes, the first and most obvious is for the protection of the human body. The second and most important is for the purpose of spiritual learning, indeed the ability to live within the immortal consciousness. Note the use of the phrase, "live within", not appreciation for, or desire to, or wish to, but, "live within."

We begin by explaining that emotions are connected to the preservation and protection of the human body, which is nothing but condensed star dust, animated by spirit or God, willed into existence as the human being. As such, the body knows the human must carry out and overcome spiritual challenges during a fairly predestined period of time in the third dimensional reality. Therefore, necessarily it has a strong desire or motivation for self preservation. The emotions vested therein are undergirded by a fear of destruction, loss of life, death. Thus, anger, hate, even love have within them elements of fear. Consider how when anger, sadness, grief or hate is experienced, there is a sense of loss that prompts those emotions. There is a feeling that something has been violated or lost or will be violated or lost, quite possibly permanently. Even when road rage is experienced, if you unbundle the experience, the rager is demonstrating an extremely strong energy because he or she feels that in some way something fundamental has been violated by the ragee, the one that is being raged upon.

Just a few days ago, Gregory noticed he was being tailgated just before he was slowing to make a right turn into a shopping center entrance. The automobile behind him swerved immediately left to pass him and then swerved in front of him to turn into the same entrance. He very nearly broadsided the car. The driver, a woman, rushed into a nearby pharmacy where she waited for a prescription. Gregory walked up to her and said quietly: "Madam, on behalf of the general public, I would like to ask you to drive more carefully. Your driving is very dangerous." She did not look up or speak.

Shortly thereafter, Gregory was surprised to see the woman approach him in the store next to the pharmacy. She said very angrily, "You told ME I was a bad driver. You are a bad driver, driving 20 miles an hour in a 40 mile an hour zone." Gregory responded calmly, "I did not say you were a bad driver. I said you were a dangerous driver. There is a difference." She angrily turned and stormed out of the store.

The purpose this example is to neither praise Gregory nor to condemn the woman driver. It merely illustrates the threat to existence that prompts anger. In some way, the woman driver was somehow threatened by an automobile moving to make a turn more slowly than she thought proper and risked being broadsided by Gregory's car, which was turning into the same entrance. Had that occurred, the seconds she gained would have been lost waiting for the police, an ambulance and a tow truck. There's no telling what would have been lost had she been injured.

The range of emotions that humans are given provides an opportunity to recognize them in their occurrence and to moderate, if not modulate, their expression. In the third dimensional world, however, the greatest learning is of emotional neutrality, as we have said elsewhere. However, what we did not emphasize is the importance of recognizing not only the circumstances, in which they appear, but also their tone and tenor. This experience and the ability to practice neutrality in their presence is all that is needed or expected.

In the higher domains, human emotions will be shown to be precursors of energetic relations and interdimensional experiences necessary to the continuity of immortality, and more importantly, the fuller manifestation of the Creator throughout those worlds in which one is privileged to serve. For these and other reasons, many teachers and masters have emphasized detachment or non-attachment. The truth of the matter is that full absorption in the Creator is the only focus to have. With detachment and non-attachment, the emphasis is still on the object of attachment or detachment. When the attention is fully on being one with the Creator, detachment and non-attachment are not only unimportant, they are irrelevant.

The Light Givers

GOLDEN AGE LIGHT GIVER MESSAGE 8

—◯◯◯—

Gregory: What wisdom do you have for ME now?

Ra: I am Ra. We wish to speak to you now about living the life of Spirit. Much has been written about living the life of Spirit, allowing Spirit to flow. The problem with that perspective is that it conjures an image of one being completely hollow with spirit flowing, somewhat like a stream, through the individual, presumably pouring out into life. This image is completely incorrect. The fact is that when Spirit truly flows, it animates every single aspect of the individual, so the body, mind, emotions, memory and every single aspect of the individual is completely consumed, if not transformed, by the spirit.

The irony is that Spirit is completely poised within the individual for total expression. The problem is that the distortion of life, internal and external, fears, worries, anger, attachment and ego all combine to subvert, if not prevent the flow of Spirit. When things occur within the physical and psychological environment of the individual, quite often as if they are the shutter of a camera, the very aperture through which life is seen very nearly closes and only a small drop of spirit puddles. The remainder lies fallow within the individual, completely unexpressed. How many people accept the small amount of spirit that slips through as the true essence of how spirit manifests itself in life? What a pity! In fact, rather than a small spurt, how spirit should emerge should be in the form of a geyser that soaks the individual and swirls and splashes all within his presence. This should be so much so that those nearby should be able to say to themselves: *The Presence is here; I do feel the Spirit; I am truly uplifted*.

In some traditions, the higher awareness is spoken of as being in the bliss state. What does this mean? It means being so filled with feelings of joy and exaltation that one feels happy without reason. This is the essence of the Spirit-filled state. Almost all people feel joyous at one time or another, but in most cases they are easily able to point to some event, some person, some reason, something that sparked the joy. The problem with such moments is that just as they come, they are sure to go. Why? Because such experiences are merely reflections of being in the third dimensional world where each exists in contrast to its direct opposite.

This holds true, not only for actions, but also so emotions. So, within the seed of every action, there is the seed of its opposing action. And, in the seed of every emotion there is the seed of the opposite emotion. Thus, within joy in the third-dimensional world, there is sadness. Within love, there is hate. The anger divorcees often feel toward their former spouse bears witness to the hate or anger buried within third-dimensional love. If one learns to allow spirit to truly animate their life, they come to the point where they realize that nothing is of greater importance than surrendering all of the distortions that tend to impede the flow and true realization of spirit, so that the vision of others, the tendencies of oneself, and the aspirations that one has completely integrate themselves into the flow.

Most people live their lives in stops and starts, in moves and repose. Imagine, if you will, living a life of continuous flow: where even in stillness, the spirit moves; and even in motion, spirit moves. Where life is a continuous rhapsody of spiritual love. The fall of a leaf. The chirp of a bird. Even the buzz of a mosquito. Where one comes to the point to understand, truly understand that the greatest gift of spirit is not just to know you are spirit, but to be spirit actualized, in daily life.

So, to complete the metaphor, rather than seeing life in which spirit dribbles and drips through the human existence, life must be seen as if one is living in a torrent, a veritable downpour, a continuous stream pouring itself into and through all life, like a magnificent flood, submerging, soaking and even submerging to the very depths of Source, all who come in contact with it, whether they know it or not.

The Light Givers

GOLDEN AGE LIGHT GIVER MESSAGE 9

—✺—

Gregory: What wisdom do you have for me?

We are the Light Givers: Today, we will speak of blessing. All religions and spiritual paths include within them some form of blessing. But just what is blessing? It is the intentional outflow of spiritual energy with the aim and net effect of upliftments. More importantly, blessing is the sharing of spiritual energy aimed at uplifting and transcending beyond whatever obstacles appear to be in one's path. It is the mutual exchange of such energy that makes blessing such a unique transaction. In the moment that blessing is done, the highest aspect of one's self actually transmits and receives spiritual energy. There is greeting, "Namaste," which means the highest aspect of MY self greets and celebrates the highest aspect of yourself to which the response is "Namaste," with the same meaning. Blessing carries the same meaning as well, even though the words spoken might be different, such as "I bless you."

We are using this example because many people learn to bless each other "in the name of some higher being." What that does is rob the one who is blessing of the direct exchange of spiritual energy. When "I bless you" is said, it activates the Source energy within the individual's field and opens a profound spiritual connection between him and whomever he is blessing. In that moment, one might say there is a tremendous download of spiritual energy that opens between the individual and the person who is being blessed, so there is truly a spiritual benefit, just by saying "I bless you." If what is said is in the name of someone or something else, then the giver of the blessing is deprived of the spiritual download and benefits of blessing. While the recipient will receive the blessing energy, the giver of the blessing deprives him of what is rightfully his to enjoy. Thus, we strongly advise to always personalize blessing. The word "I" does not have to be said. Even just saying, "Bless you" implies and personalizes the blessing.

In that connection, we recommend that you may find your life enhanced in fairly unimaginable ways, by on a regular basis saying inwardly to Source, "Source, I bless you and thank you for all." If you even experiment with that statement, you will notice quite a download of blessing energy that lifts you practically into a transcendent state of being. Obstacles, delays and interruptions in your life will become almost transparent to you. The way will be made clear to you, so that even if life pretends to be burdensome, the spiritual opportunities will be even more apparent. Others around you will not understand how you are able to radiate such a profound sense of peace and comfort when others, in similar situations, would be extremely upset, disturbed and angry. Not you, because you are surrounded and filled with Source and, in that moment, are blessing the entire universe. Most importantly, the universe is blessing you and you are blessing it.

Bless ever single thought, every single thing that appears in your vision; bless everyone you know, all disasters, wars, violent acts and individuals. Bless all. If you are able to do this continuously, you will soon find that you are living in a sea of continuous blessing, awash in divine energy and that blessing energy is pouring through and to you bringing you into the state experienced by those known down through the ages as saints or holy men. Oh, precious delight, to live in a state of holy devotion, knowing that you yourself are now a blessing upon the world. We do bless you! Be in a state of continuous blessing. Bless you and bless all.

The Light Givers

GOLDEN AGE LIGHT GIVER MESSAGE 10

Light Givers: In the last three dictations in this series, we will share previously dictated information that was originally intended for a yet to be developed booklet on Ascension. In the meantime, we hope these answers to commonly asked questions will be helpful.

What is Ascension?

Ascension is a permanent condition. It is the never-ending unfoldment of consciousness that begins with the harmonizing of an element to its external environment. What is not clear to many, however, is the fact that it is not simply achieved on one's own merit. It is always achieved via the grace of a higher being or some great master who is empowered to transmit Ascension energy. Much like the electrons that move from a lower orbit to one higher and release enormous amounts of energy, the individual consciousness does not transit from one level to another without an assisting burst of Ascension energy. This is a point known, but not well understood. Ascension, pure and simple, is not simply based on one's individual effort. It comes as a function of the recognition and reward for such effort and can thereby be granted.

What are the different types of Ascension?

There are three main types of Ascension: spiritual, physical and extraterrestrial. First and foremost is what could be called spiritual ascension. This is the conscious expansion and transmigration of the individual's sense of self, both in terms of being and location, from one domain of experience and interaction to another. While this requires a degree of disciplined behavior in preparation for Ascension, it does not occur with energetic transmissions from an individual already vested with Ascension energy.

The second, and closely related, is physical ascension. This is the transformation of the individual's various energy bodies vibrationally to frequencies outside the range of human seeing and hearing. In each experience, individuals learn how to adjust and readjust their frequencies so that they can be visible to, and interact with beings who exist within available ranges. Both require considerable discipline, both to achieve and maintain.

However, the discipline required for physical ascension is much greater, in that in addition to the meditations and contemplations of spiritual ascension, the individual who aspires to physical ascension must be willing to adopt a level of ascetic practice seldom experienced in modern times and exclude practically all other aspects of human life. Most accounts of physical ascension involve mastery of the art of living on light, pure solar energy, and the separation, practically, from most normal human activities and functions. This is a noble undertaking to which few aspire, however.

There are accounts of individuals who remained in dark confined areas for years as part of their effort to achieve this state. There are also accounts of individuals who used extreme fasting methods. The secret to Ascension is that the individual is basically learning to, and experiencing the total relocation of his internal referents. Jesus spoke of this as the Kingdom of Heaven; Buddha, used non-attachment as a key referent, even though the void is where the Buddhist aims for relocation; but the central point is that the personal reference is shifted.

Other teachers have spoken of it in various ways. In the Universal Healer, we speak of higher and infinite domains. This point cannot be overemphasized enough. So, rather than being here looking up, you are here, looking down, as it were. More importantly, to all intents and purposes, the process of Ascension is unending and goes beyond eternity. The question most people face is whether they wish to live out their incarnated cycle with the worlds of matter, energy, space and time as their principal reference or would they prefer to live in an Ascended state, knowing full well that their existence here is basically a transient phenomenon.

Extraterrestrial Ascension is principally concerned with movement into higher vibrations through the actions of beings from other planets or dimensions. There is an extent to which this is similar to physical ascension, in terms of the outcomes. What is different is that the prime movers are the technologies managed and controlled by others. In some scenarios, this involves being physically transported in extraterrestrial vehicles and so on. There is a second consideration and that is whether or not dependence on external technologies, or individuals, for that matter, aligns fully with the goal of spiritual evolution. Clearly, it is a matter of personal choice and of no concern to God or Source itself. What does it matter if many eons pass before the individual takes up again his journey to the heart of the Creator.

Why is there such an interest in Ascension today?

The interest in Ascension today is no greater than the interest has always been. However, with greater literacy, the public nature of various spiritual practices, the greater economic freedoms that result in more leisure time, it is possible for many, many more people to pursue questions related to spiritual growth, advanced healing and Ascension. The problem is that Ascension has been camouflaged and restricted for such a long time that many people are not able to distinguish between what

Ascension truly offers and what they believe they are receiving or will receive via their traditional religious practices or alternative spiritual paths. Here's the story. Christianity holds out the vision of Ascension as the phenomenon witnessed by the Apostles, i.e., Jesus being lifted into heaven out of their sight. Implicitly, such ascension was available only to Jesus, leaving most Christians to look forward to ascension after death or when Christ returns, depending upon the particular Christian religion.

In other traditions, there is complete acceptance of the idea of the inner Ascension, i.e., the movement and relocation of the consciousness into the immortal state. As it happens, such an experience, while secretly longed for, has been and is reserved to the Master and/or his successor. Others, while just as devoted, disciplined, and devout, cannot hope for such, on a sustained basis, because they have not been chosen. The Master is, essentially, worshipped as a living example of the possibility of Ascension, but there is a dim likelihood of being granted that or entering that state on a sustained basis, without spending many hours in contemplation, meditation or prayer. Yet one cannot examine any religious or spiritual practice without finding substantial evidence of an overwhelming interest in the Ascended state, however limited the actual achievement has been.

What is the spiritual nature of the individual?

This is an interesting question, one that has received millions of pages of attention, down through the ages, quite typically by those who have received enlightenment. MY answer will be simple. The individual is like the leaf on the branch of the tree. Is the leaf defined by its purpose, i.e., to serve as a collector of sunlight, carbon dioxide, and other nutrients? Is the leaf defined by the greater function of the tree? The Forest? The location of the Forest? The Continent? The Planet? Or vice versa? Likewise, is the individual defined by his greater functions? Yes, to the extent he accepts the spiritual capacity to operate and experience himself in those greater functions as his self-referents. But it is all hopeless wishing, without the energetic support to sustain his awareness at those levels.

Rather than puzzling over this metaphor to agree or disagree, a better use of one's time is to determine what needs to be done in order to accept Ascension. This is a very important point. Most read the words of enlightenment, written while in the Ascended state, as if understanding the thought is the same as experiencing the conditions that produced the thought. Other's thoughts are only the shadows of reality. Reality for you is the direct experience of the conditions that produced the thought.

So, the rhapsodies, sonnets, essays, books, and many, many writings are but echoes of the enlightened realities that produced them. They are the faint indications of the possibilities that can only be entered temporarily via meditation, contemplation, prayer and the other worshipful arts. To be sustained and live in that consciousness is yet another matter. That is desired, aimed for, hoped for, and even wished for, but in order for that to occur, the secret that has been in plain sight for such a long time, is that some Being has to help. That's all there is to it. Nothing more. Nothing less.

Thus, it makes sense to pray for God's grace, to entreat the Archangels and Saints, to beseech God in prayer, as many have done, down through the ages. And, it explains why the accounts of every great being always include becoming filled with the light or being blessed by their teacher. It is only man's conceit and ego that would make him think that what is achieved via healing or spirituality is by the dint of his own efforts.

The Light Givers

GOLDEN AGE LIGHT GIVER MESSAGE 11

How does one prepare oneself for Ascension?

Preparation for Ascension is a natural process of spiritual and healing evolution. It is the development of the ability to live in a continuous state of joy and bliss. So many teachers have spent their entire lives helping individuals to prepare for ascension with tips and coaching about how to eat, pray, speak, think, meditate, contemplate, exercise, and, in one word – live. What is not clear to most is that what lies underneath all of the direction that one receives are recommendations that lead to being single-minded. Driving an automobile is an excellent example. A driver risks himself and his passengers if he is all over the road, swerving, making u-turns, stopping without warning and so on. The individual who wishes to Ascend without discipline likewise places himself and others at risk.

How? The wisdom, knowledge and spiritual and healing energy that comes to the Ascended consciousness is of such a nature that, without the capacity to be single-minded, one can become unbalanced and of little use to himself or others. To extend the point, one of the intentions of Ascension is to enhance the individual's ability to participate fully in normal daily life and, at the same time, partake or exist in higher states of awareness and beingness. For many spiritual and healing orders, this ability is highly prized and seen, quite frankly, as being the sole purpose of life and living. In other words, as has been said many times, many ways, to be in the world, but not of it. Consequently, what is taught and practiced by them has the essential aim of sharpening the individual's focus, single-mindedness, and narrowing the attention to the exclusion of the more distracting elements of existence.

What are the benefits?

The benefits of Ascension are countless. Perhaps the main benefit of Ascension is the recognition and achievement of what could be called the Divine context. Many people spend their entire lives reading, studying and listening to enlightened individuals who talk and write about the overall purpose of life and how we all fit into it. Hours and hours, days and days, years and years are taken up in rapt attention, as if by cramming the information into our skulls, we will somehow make the transition. Yet it does not occur.

The benefits of Ascension are quite simple and many. What has eluded us becomes ours: the expanded consciousness, the bliss state, the tranquility, the God wisdom, and so on. Perhaps the most important benefit is that we finally get it. It all makes sense. We do understand it, in a way that we could not possibly have understood it before, because we were not in it. It's comparable to a desert nomad, who lives in a world of limitless sand where water is a scarce commodity trying to truly understand the concept of an ocean of limitless salt water. Plunge him into the ocean and he gets it in a moment. Such is the benefit of Ascension. There is a solitariness, indeed, a singularity of consciousness that is well worth Being.

Is there a secret society of Ascenders?

There are many such societies of Ascenders, some of which have been in existence down through the ages. In some cases, they have taken the form of spiritual orders. In others, healing societies and practitioners. What has been kept from the public at large is the role that Ascenders have played in the perpetuation of the practice and in the transmission of the energies associated with Ascension. It cannot be overstated that one cannot simply ascend on his or her own. The most one can do is prepare for Ascension, that is to say, do as much as one can in preparation. But the fundamental act of Ascension is facilitated by the conscious attention of one who has within the empowerment to provide such assistance to the individual who has that intention. Ascension requires not only acceptance but also intention to be in the Ascended state. It is much like the art of bike-riding. We can place someone on a bike as much as we wish. But if he has no intention of remaining in that position, he will quickly plummet to the earth.

What is the role of the Source in Ascension?

This is an excellent question (not that the others aren't). Not only is this an excellent question, this is the key question. The Source is the principal vehicle by which Ascension occurs and to which Ascension directs. Those empowered with the power to perform Ascensions are not only embued with Source energy, but they are energetically the source of it themselves. Mark these words, they are the Source itself. Not only is their intention and that of the Source coincident but energetically, they and the Source are one. This point cannot be overemphasized. Thus, it is simply by the gentle power of intention that the Ascension experience is granted. Accordingly, in the Universal Healer system, Ascension is brought about in connection with the domain to which the Archangels have assigned his respective Ascension ability.

Is there any limit to Ascension?

To all extents and purposes, Ascension is limitless. The Universe is a multifaceted, timeless, limitless experience. Indeed, the concept of limit truly has no meaning outside of the worlds of time and space. Indeed, Ascension itself loses its early meaning and comes to stand for something else, that being, the completely transformative and transformed nature of consciousness and the immutable and permeable nature of reality in the context of union and interaction with other intelligences and sentient beings. The process is one of continuous finding, of entering and interpenetrating expanding and contracting forms of awareness and Beingness, of connecting and disconnecting, of entering and exiting, of being the one among the many, the many within the one, the one within the many, the continuous within the discontinuous, the discontinuous within the continuous and so on. The role of those who perform Ascensions, both on the inner and the outer, such as the Grand Master, is to support the energetic transitions associated with Ascension to the extent that they do occur.

What is the role of extraterrestrials in Ascension?

There is much that has been recorded about the role of extraterrestrials in Ascension; some of it has been good and some has been bad. Yet even the word, "extraterrestrials," insufficiently anticipates what most needs to be understood, that being that everything in the universe is extraterrestrial, except what occurs on this tiny mud ball called Earth. God is extraterrestrial. To the extent he is the Son of God, Jesus is extraterrestrial. Archangels and angels are extraterrestrial. Every person born into this word is extraterrestrial because, prior to reincarnation, they were somewhere outside of the normal field of consciousness. Thus, they were "extra", which means outside, "terrestrial", planet Earth. So, by definition, extraterrestrial is a xenophobic term.

To recast the question, do beings who did not originate on Earth have a role in Ascension? Yes, their roles vary, depending upon their intention and responsibilities. The internet is replete with accounts of fleets from other galaxies that visited Earth in centuries past and that are currently in the solar system. Ancient Ascended Masters, Archangels and other Beings purportedly of Divine origin have long histories of contact with various individuals, some recorded, some not. Whether or not any of these individuals will either restore heaven on earth, conduct mass migrations, or place the Earth's inhabitants in some sort of galactic concentration or rehabilitation camp, remains to be seen. (Some say that the Earth is already a galactic rehabilitation camp.)

How does the Mayan Calendar fit into this?

The Mayan calendar was an attempt by those of that time to capture what was seen through their ancient prophecies and timetables. It is a well-known fact that a great deal of accuracy has been accorded to the Calendar's results and many have been astounded by the precision of its forecasts. What many have questioned and somewhat feared is how the Calendar has no predictions beyond 2012. For many, this augurs the expectations of the world ending via some great cataclysm and that, like the dinosaurs, the human beings vanish from the face of the Earth and await repopulation by some alien race. Indeed, there are accounts by some of this happening during prehistoric times with repopulation of the planet being conducted by space travelers. The explanation for the Mayan Calendar's ending at 2012 is simply that 2012 was as far, vibrationally, as they could reach. To be sure, the Earth will move through a vortex around that time, a vortex that will be little noticed by the people of earth. However, the time travelers of the Mayan period were simply unable to make the energetic shift. So, to them, for all intents and purposes, the Earth vanished. It no more vanished than did the stars and galaxies now being accessed via the Hubble telescope.

Prior to Hubble, the vision of those on this planet imply did not reach that far. The vision of the Mayans and the other people whose calendars likewise did not record a future beyond 2012, simply did not have the reach. If anything, the Mayan Calendar is proof that the human being has had a capacity that has yet to be systematically achieved by most people today. Also, falling into this camp was Nostradamus. Nostradamus was an extraordinary scientist, visionary, prophet and even soothsayer. He mastered early on the science and application of herbs, forecasting via time travel that allowed him to see into the future. He, like the Mayans, had a profound interest in understanding not only what was happening in his time, but also what was to occur in the future. He had a great love for all life and was delighted by the idea that someday all humans would be able to incorporate into their lives the skills and abilities he experienced. It is a perspective to which he devoted his life. The predictions that have come true have largely fallen into the area of calamities and disasters, earning him the nickname, prophet of doom.

The Light Givers

GOLDEN AGE LIGHT GIVER MESSAGE 12

How does the Ascended person fit into daily life?

This is a question that is fundamental to understanding the true essence of Ascension. There are many that assume that, with the Ascended consciousness, one should distance himself, in the name of detachment, from daily life. Oh no, the truly Ascended person can plunge directly into all matter of affairs and activities on a regular and daily basis. Who better exemplifies the nature of the Ascended individual than Rumi, the famed Sufi master and poet? He taught at more than one university, consumed great volumes of wine and probably never turned down a good argument or fight. Yet he lived a life of MY stery, passion and adventure, completely immersed in all the aspects of living. Who better to be involved directly in all of life's adventures than one that knows life is truly an illusion and not the ultimate reality. The truly Ascended person is able to penetrate more quickly to that which is true and good and which is able to uplift the individual consciousness from the muck and mire of daily life, which leads to the next question.

What must be the focus of the Ascended individual?

The Ascended individual has a solitary focus. And, that is upon the twin themes of Source and his continued transformation into the essence of it. All other foci, albeit important, are ephemeral and of passing interest. There is a permanence to the focus upon source that is more than simply being transcendent. The very notion of transcendence acknowledges a relationship between a presumed experience that is greater or more than something else. The truth of the matter is that with the focus on Source, one comes to realize that there truly IS nothing else other than Source. To experience Source is not merely transcendent, it is transformational in that one becomes more aware of what he is, not what he was or what he will be, but what he IS. And, that is, that he is composed of the same material, as it were, that God IS. And that the life or lives he has been given have been for the singular purpose of his coming to that realization. So the "continued transformation" is, in fact, "continuous realizing of one's personal divinity." With that realization things thought to be significant not only pale in comparison, they disappear. Things of importance, although given necessary attention, neither stymie not capture the permanent attention of the Ascended individual that is in this world but not of it.

How does Soul fit into Ascension?

There are two ways to consider Soul. The first way is to define it. The second way is to experience it. When defined, Soul is described as a unit of awareness, a spark of God. An even larger question is what is the purpose of Soul? Why does it exist? Soul's existence is an aspect of the limitless, unitary existence of the dynamics of the Creator God. Just as breath, oxygen, molecules and atoms are essential components of the reality of human life, so is Soul an essential component of the existence of the Creator Gods. Divine Law requires of the existence of the Creator God that it recompose the bulk of itself into units of its own awareness and undertake a Sisyphean journey of creation and recreation. It is a perpetual and universal experience that the Creator God has. One might say that it is eternal but, in fact, eternity is only an aspect of the Creator God. Thus, the experience is truly outside eternity, a concept which you humans are ill-equipped to grasp.

The process of Ascension moves through several phases, the early phases are quite linear. Subsequent phases fall under the umbrella of what some might call Quantum. The first phases precede the awareness of being human, i.e. recognition of change; recognition of self as a unitary phenomenon; recognition of feelings, emotions, attachments, etc.; and recognition of external influences upon the foregoing. The next phase is of cognitive change that includes thinking, belief, and acknowledgement of a higher power and so on. These, of course, migrate into the features of life associated with being human, such as various forms of group behavior, and are described under the heading of the evolution of culture, i.e., from hunter gathering societies all the way to modern civilization. The irony of the humanization process is that while it is civilizing and collectivizing, it is simultaneously un-individualizing. While the individual is being more aware of the group processes in which he is embedded, he has the opportunity to undergo transformation into the unitary consciousness of his Creator God. To say the process is infinite and timeless completely understates its totality.

How does karma fit into Ascension?

Karma is an essential element of the unfoldment of humanity in that it is best understood from an energetic perspective. Most people think of karma in terms of getting back the results of either what you have done or what has been done to you. Thus, negative karma occurs because you have done something bad earlier, either in this lifetime or another one. Good karma is thought to come about because of something that you have done for others, likewise in this lifetime or some other. Nothing is farther from the truth. The fact of the matter is that karma is strictly the result of mental activity and creation. It is the creation of circumstances of life that the mind extracts from its own understanding of situations and may or may not be based on specific incidents.

There are underlying energetics of karma to be understood but first, let's unbundle karma's phenomenal aspects. To be sure, there is a strong relationship between events and actions and karma. But what most do not understand is that what is known as karma is strictly a mental creation, based on individual interpretations of experiences and presumed consequences. What many are unable to do is separate the natural consequences of actions from the mental creations that surround those events with the latter serving as the basis of karma. This begs the question, the fit between karma and Ascension. Realization that karma is a mental creation is the precursor or precondition of Ascension. That realization brings a tectonic shift in the human's perception of himself in that he becomes aware that he is no longer tied to a perpetual wheel of creation. Instead, he finds that he is embedded in a transformation of greater and even great awareness, realization and Beingness that we understand as Ascension.

What brings him to this point is the acceptance of the energetic tides of life. An ocean tide simply ebbs and flows, something easily accepted. By the same token, karma is nothing but the ebb and flow of life, i.e. the actions and reactions of individuals, groups and societies, best understood as the balancing of opposing energies. The individual may simply observe those balancing of energies, free of judgment of causes, consequences, and effects, and be karma free. The individuals unable to separate themselves from the flow of matter, energy, space and time are, indeed, eternally bound to the karma wheel and are only free with the assistance of those who themselves are established outside the karmic cycle such as archangels, Ascended Masters, higher beings and others so empowered such as Mahantas, Mahatmas, Satgurus and Ascension Masters.

The simple fact is that all beings have specific points of reference or polarity points. These could be called orientation points. Most of the orientation points of humans polarize or magnetize individuals toward the wheel of karma, largely as a consequence of mental activity and personal acceptance of circumstance. Those with orientation points polarized outward to some manifestation of God or Source may be endowed with the capacity to shift one's awareness to the possibility of outward awareness. This is done with Shaktipats, initiations, deekshas, illuminated writing and so on. Thus, one's attention is focused outwardly, much as a prisoner might be on finding ways to escape once it is learned that others have gotten out in some way. Karma fits into Ascension in the following manner: it does not. Once that point is realized, one is now prepared for Ascension.

Why is realization essential for Ascension?

Realization has three components: recognition, reflection and action. Recognition is a greater event than simply observation. It involves seeing and understanding personal significance. Personal significance is what it means to the observer. Reflection is concerned with understanding its overall significance, not just to the individual, but its implications in and for the greater scheme of things. Action refers to the way in which the individual manifests the Ascended consciousness in interaction with his environments. By no means is it a passive state of existence.

This ends the first series of the Golden Age Messages. We do hope they have contributed to both the development of your understanding and your levels of spiritual awareness. Understanding here relates to your mental capacity to accept the truth of higher reality. Your spiritual awareness is directly related to your willingness to expand your capacity to experience the truths of higher reality.

The Light Givers

GOLDEN AGE LIGHT GIVER MESSAGES

2:1 - 2:12

INTELLECTUAL FREEDOM VS. SPIRITUAL FREEDOM

Elsewhere we have suggested that the best way to benefit from these dialogues is to avoid being trapped <u>within</u> the language of what is written. This may be the hardest task that you have ever faced. Why? Because the entire nature of learning through which humans go in every culture is to accept the assigned meaning of everything with which they are faced, meanings, in fact, provided by others. This is important, of course. The problem is that, the nature of learning, at least in western cultures, is to learn most things second hand. What we are referring to is what happens with schooling.

In schools, people receive the homogenized thoughts and ideas of others, most often oriented to and dominated by the ruling culture. This is not a criticism, it is merely an observation. Without such domination, human society as it exists could not exist. So, learning then typically requires surrendering curiosity, independence and intellectual freedom, which could be the gateway to spiritual freedom. Note the use of the phrase, "could be the gateway to intellectual freedom". We will return to this point later in this dictation.

So, school provides homogenized and standardized culturally dominated thinking that, without examination, is expected to be accepted as true definitions of reality. While such is understandable in a cultural context, it is practically useless in a spiritual context because the individual's own thinking processes turn inward on themselves. In a fairy tale told years ago, the hero was able to escape the dragon by tucking the dragon's tail into its mouth. The dragon thereby was destroyed because it consumed itself. You may not believe the fairy tale, but the way in which the application of schooling to spiritual topics turns thinking inward is not unlike the dragon's self-destruction.

The question we raise here revisits the question of how best to benefit from these materials. Is it by trying to memorize key phrases, ideas, concepts and constructions? Is it by regurgitating words and ideas? Is it by consuming the material rapidly and eagerly awaiting the opportunity to read more. None of these.

Earlier, we mentioned that intellectual freedom could be the gateway to spiritual freedom. Let us unbundle this point. First, what is spiritual freedom? To our way of thinking, spiritual freedom is that which occurs when you come to the realization that life is one of limitless possibilities. Spiritual freedom is truly experienced when you are able to step out of the box of commonly accepted truths and ideas. It is when you are willing to experience wisdom as the direct result of your interactions with life as it is. Intellectual freedom can be a bridge in an oddly indirect way. And, it does this when you realize that you have reached the limits of what you can know based on your own review of others' writings and ideas. It is when you understand that direct experience is the only authentic source of spiritual wisdom and growth.

At this point, it does not mean that someone is going to bestow upon you a million opportunities. What it means is that, in your heart of hearts, you know, not believe, not want, not hope, you know that you are unlimited and occupy space, we'll say in a limitless and unbounded universe. By definition, what is lived in is an omniverse, which, by, or indeed, absent definition, is way beyond the scope of a "universe." To expand this point, by contrast, have you known individuals that lived in a "yes, but" universe, people who lived as if no good could ever come to them? In fact, their belief that no good could come to them was or is so strong, that sure enough, no good ever came or comes to them. What their attention was on magnified exponentially, indeed, overwhelming their lives.

Paul Twitchell, the great Eckankar founder, titled the first book that came to readers' attention, "In MY Soul, I am Free." This is the fundamental perspective of spiritual freedom.

Therefore, we ask that, while it might be somewhat comforting to align your perceptions of spiritual reality with the words and ideas we share with you in the dictations, please do not confine your reflections, realizations and recognitions to the words on these pages. Notice how some of these ideas may resonate with you, how some may remind you of topics that first appear almost unrelated, or how your attention may shift subtly inward, not further into the textual material, but into an inner or outer reality that may seem to be wanting to burst through in both a non-local or neo-local way. How exciting!

Up to this point, we have limited our comments to the ways in which you might approach this material. What we have saved for last is consideration of the role a spiritual teacher must play in loosening the bonds of schooling upon the way in which his own teachings are considered. First this teaching must avoid expounding and pontificating, if at all possible. If not, rather than narrowing the distance between the teacher and his students, the spiritual gap is widened. This broadens the distance spiritually between the teacher and his students, by the perceived "expertise" of the teacher. The truth of the matter is that the teacher's only expertise is the ability to think his own thoughts, which may or may not be particularly relevant for his students. In fact, because they are only his thoughts, the likelihood is that his thoughts are completely irrelevant. Much as these thoughts here are truly irrelevant.

Secondly, the teacher must avoid correcting or redirecting the focus of the students' thinking. Instead the teacher should follow and be catalyzed by the students' thinking.

Thirdly, the teacher must support and encourage thinking that is independent of outside direction. Fourth, the master's contributions should largely be questions intended to unlock or bridge the gap from the gates of intellectual thought to the gates of spiritual thought.

Intellectual thought is by definition bounded by rules, understandings and frameworks. Spiritual thought has no such boundaries and is best understood only when reflecting relationships to Source. If directionality is used to distinguish the two, intellectual thought is largely horizontal, involving comparisons between and among parallel ideas. Spiritual reality might be considered to be expansive, broadly inclusive, reflecting solely the relationship of one to the One in a non-directional way.

Thus, the teacher, by his silence, affirms the spiritual freedom of all in discussion with him. However, we expect him to vigilantly protect and provide the opportunity for each to have a voice in the discussion, no matter how unrelated the comment may appear to be. By definition, nothing said sincerely could ever be unrelated to the true nature of unbounded spiritual reality.

GOLDEN AGE #2/MESSAGE 2:

LIVING THE INSPIRED LIFE

The nature of the human consciousness is to have its ups and downs, moments of happiness and moments of sadness. For many, this is a fairly natural state of being, so much so that friends and family members sometimes tremble, wondering how they and others feel on a day to day basis. Even though this is the normal human condition for many, it is a sad state of affairs. Why is it sad? Because what it takes to be in a regular, joyous state has been given already.

There's a great story called, "Acres of Diamonds." The way the story goes is the following. A man owned acres of land covered with rocks of various sizes, so many in fact that the land was worthless to him. He finally sold the land for little or no money and took off on a worldwide adventure seeking to make his fortune.

Years later, after failing to achieve his dream, he returned to the area where he sold his original plot of land. He was amazed to see that the individual who had purchased the land from him was fabulously wealthy. He asked, "What happened?" "Did you strike oil? Dig up gold?" The answer he heard was "Remember all those worthless rocks on this property?" "Yes," he answered. "Well, they are diamonds, acres and acres of diamonds!"

The meaning of this story is quite clear: all that we need is already present. We just need to have the foresight and vision to recognize what is already given us.

So, being able to live in a continuous state of joy is a gift we already have. What is needed is the capacity to recognize the gift and apply it to our daily lives. There is a gospel song, of which Gregory is quite fond, titled, "I Won't Complain." The singer chronicles a list of ailments and difficulties that seem impossible to overcome and after each item on the list, he sings "I won't complain," adding, "Thank you, Lord." What comes through, almost as an undertone, is the singer's tremendous spiritual strength and his strong reliance on God for life's successes and his unwillingness to see anything that occurs as life's failures.

So, in a real sense every obstacle or difficulty with which he is faced is simply another of God's diamonds which, if cracked open, will be revealed as a gift. So, what are the diamonds in your life? Can you open your spiritual senses to understand the many gifts that you have been given? Can you say with meaning and conviction for each, "I won't complain" and "Thank you, Lord."

THE MIRACLE OF LIFE

In this dictation, we wish to address the miracle and gift that life truly is. Now many people live their lives as if a great burden has been placed upon them. Troubles, disappointments and despair practically overwhelm them. What is lost sight of by so many is that life itself is a miracle.

Most people think of a miracle as something fairly dramatic, even stupendous; but, if you stop and think, merely being able to rest aware or unaware and then to wake up to life is purely nothing short of miraculous. Moreover, it is truly miraculous to come to the understanding that life as it is, is a direct function of the way that we see it.

This point underscores the relationship between the world we experience and the way we view the world. If an individual is filled with fear for no good reason, then the life he lives is a fearful one. By no means is this to minimize the absolute terror in which some live because of the criminality of their neighborhoods or the lack of safety in the streets.

But, all things being equal, there are many individuals who experience difficulties that you might not associate with fear: anger, hurt, sadness, hypersensitivity and so on. Under each of these emotions is a subconscious fear of non-survival, of being obliterated and even of being found inconsequential. This explains why so many people, rather than rejoicing that each day provides yet another opportunity to experience life, love and happiness, wake up instead dreading every step of the day.

The true miracle of human existence is to recognize the relationship between how one experiences the world and how one views the world. Nothing makes this point better than to see and experience the changes that come about because of prayer, intentional meditation, contemplation or the services provided by one that is filled with the Holy Spirit. In his e-book, *The Universal Healer: God Energy in Action – A handbook for Advanced Healing*, Gregory writes words to the effect that the true purpose of healing is to actively demonstrate that a change in consciousness can bring about a change in one's reality, whether it is to lessen a headache, repair a wound, to remedy the results of past or this life trauma or even experience the Kingdom of Heaven.

Those that call themselves healers and presume that what occurs is the result of their actions are foolish, indeed. The fact of the matter is that God and God alone via His designees, such as Jesus, the Archangels and a few selected individuals like Gregory, is the true healer. The most the healer can do is serve as a viewpoint that locates the recipient or client in time and space. The correct attitude is that of Jesus: "It is not I that doeth the work, but it is the Father within me."

The Universal Healer practitioner is an excellent example of this at work. To become a UH practitioner requires not only some familiarity with healing modalities, but, more importantly, it requires the willingness to be open to Universal Healing and to know that while he or she is managing or leading the recipient through the stages of the treatment, it is not the healer that does the work, it is the Divine within.

The UH practitioner is mindful that the recipient receives the healing of a more permanent character, based upon the recipient's faith in God. To repeat, the permanence of the healing depends upon one's faith in God. Moreover, Divine law requires that the recipient accept the responsibility for maintaining the faith and continuing his prayers, meditations and contemplations.

There is a sense that the UH healing brings the individual completely into balance like a spinning gyroscope, but to maintain the balance, freedom of choice must be exercised to maintain the healed condition. Should the balance be lost, the recipient may ask God, Jesus, the holy angels, or some other God appointed and anointed individual he looks to, to have mercy upon him. That request needs to be followed up with routine spiritual practice, whether it is prayer, contemplation, meditation, Tai Chi or some other internal art.

The true miracle is experienced with the awakening from the oppressive nature of daily life to the joy of Soul awareness, of coming to understand that, despite the limitations of daily life, in God's eyes, you are truly unlimited. This is a wonderful realization and something to be believed. But more than that, the healing provides you with the opportunity of a lifetime, a genuine transformation of consciousness that is truly an awakening. Life itself is a miracle indeed.

SECRETS OF THE GOD BEING

In this dictation, we explore the hidden world of the true God Being. We plan to be less flowery and exalted in our language than is typical of those that explore an esoteric topic as this. History is replete with examples of men and women that truly lived within the God force and were well recognized as God in the flesh or God Beings. And, history is filled with their utterances, exaltations, speeches and sermons. What is less well understood is the nature of their inner life and a clear understanding of what drove and what drives them, present company included.

While to most people the focus of attention on such spiritual beings is upon their godliness, the truth of the matter is that they were centered, as well, almost as much, in daily life: attending to family, personal matters, personal hygiene and such drew their attention as much as it did their neighbors. Nevertheless, to accomplish their spiritual missions and to inspire their followers, devotees and students, the bulk of their time with them was spent on exploring, presenting and demonstrating the higher truths. If you stop to think about it, this makes perfect sense. Given that God fills the entire universe with consciousness, love and awareness, would it not follow that the true God person must be fully present in daily life?

So, you may ask, is the "God person" just pretending to be centered in God? Absolutely not. In a sense, he is co-present, in that he is in full expression in God and in full expression in daily life. To be sure, in order to achieve this state, there are periods in which he is consciously absent from the rigors of daily life via prayer, meditation, Tai Chi, yoga and retreats of varying types and lengths. What distinguishes him is confidence and courage by which he lives life and his willingness to be always alert to the ways in which distractions interfere. Doubt, disappointment and discouragement do not plague his existence.

Now, please understand. Do not think that he does not have his moments. Did not Jesus in the garden at Gethsemane ask God to remove the "bitter cup?" But, even then, he shortly thereafter surrendered to the will of God and carried out his spiritual mission that included the crucifixion. Understand, the crucifixion was not his spiritual mission. There were many being crucified by the Romans during those days. His mission was to demonstrate the continuity of Life and to hold before mankind the impermanence of sin and bring to all the experience God's eternal forgiveness.

Recast in the language more familiar to the readers, Jesus is a living example of the continuity of human consciousness and the capacity to transform and be transformed into a true Divine Being. Did he not tell his disciples that they would be able to perform the same works as he? Did he not say, "The Kingdom of Heaven is within?" Did he not say that, "The Father and I are One." While Jesus should certainly be venerated and respected because he carried out his spiritual mission in such a grand fashion, we lose sight of the true message of his life, if we resort to worshipping him. He gave the world, as it has been preserved by the western culture, a clear example of how we might likewise be manifestations of God.

And how is that? By doing the necessary work to minimize the ways which distract us from the many ways in which Divinity shows up in daily life. What is required is something akin to vigilance, in terms of noticing how distractions show up to interfere in our relationship to God. Note the paradigm shift. It begins with the understanding that it is completely natural to be aware of God's presence. But our senses are drawn away to the movement, activity and interactions of the external world, shifting our spiritual awareness away.

Be aware that the natural tendency of the human mind is to focus on details. The natural tendency of the spiritual mind is to unfocus and to be aware of insights and wisdom that reveal the spiritual context in which reality expresses itself. In other words, if your attention, even in reviewing this message, rests or centers upon detail, in a real sense, you are looking in the wrong place. What you may do in every circumstance is relax your attention, be aware of noticing your inner awareness and be open to whatever wisdom shows up.

As you undertake the transformation into the God Being, will you need to be crucified? Probably not. But you may have a few uncomfortable moments with friends and relatives. To further this point, notice the one or two ideas that seem the most important to you. Hold those thoughts and notice how the awareness of God creeps into your consciousness. Be one with it. Therein begins the unfolding of the true secret of the God Being. Do not feel envy, awe or worship for him that has experienced or is experiencing this state. For the emotions of envy and awe are what form the fabric of cults and religions that ensnare followers in the folds of the robes of their leaders.

Instead, let the experience of God expand your spiritual freedom in an uncompromising way. True God awareness is your birthright and we and Gregory are fully committed to supporting you as you embrace it. You are the God Being incarnate. As such, you are becoming continually aware of the ways in which God interpenetrates life and how you are nothing but an expression of it. Hold that thought.

GOLDEN AGE #2/MESSAGE 5

WHAT IS YOUR SPIRITUAL PURPOSE?

This is a question that many have pondered for centuries. It is an age old concern that man must face, given his construction as a human being. There is no evidence that any other creatures on the planet ponder, save, quite possibly dolphins with their highly developed brains. It is ingrained into the human DNA, the search for meaning in life, which should by definition transport the individual from living in a highly reactive, troubled, turbulent environment. Yet, most humans do not spend their lives looking for their spiritual purpose. We suspect that the question lingers yet for even those on their death beds. Why was I born? What was MY life's purpose? What happens now? Even though it is commonly known and remarked, "No one on their death bed thinks 'I wish I had spent more time in the office'." Here's a bit of advice that might be a bit more death bed appropriate. "Thank you, Lord, for giving ME yet another lifetime to expand MY self in your love."

This thought, albeit somewhat corny, is closer to the last expression that we think one should have during his transition from this vibration. Note the use of the word, "transition." That's a fairer representation of what death truly is. One merely transitions from this world of vibrations to a higher and less dense vibratory reality. Freed of the vibrations of the physical body and its attendant energy body, one's Soul Awareness re-centers itself, for some momentarily or even longer, prior to reincarnating to experience yet again another lifetime to expand in God's love.

This may seem an oversimplification, i.e., the purpose of life being to expand more deeply in God's love. But if you stop and think about all the reasons given for being on the planet and the ways in which spiritual teachers, gurus and others have talked about how life should be lived, i.e., love ye one another, treat your neighbor as you wish to be treated, God is love, and so on, what is a better way to describe the purpose of life? How many memorials, monuments and holidays are erected and celebrated for reasons that are dimly remembered.

Washington D.C. is replete with monuments and statues to long forgotten heroes. These are individuals whose purposes seem to have been immortalized by those who commissioned and erected statues on their behalf. Yet if you were able to interview them and asked them what their spiritual purpose was, the odds are that they would not identify any of the reasons that led to their memorialization. The odds are that they would identify some aspect of their lives in which love was the greatest expression.

What is your spiritual purpose in life? How are you doing with it? Are things so tumultuous that you have not been able to put your attention on it? How is that possible? Is your life so chaotic that you are unable to go out your door fully dressed? Is it so overwhelming that you don't remember how to start your car, to use its brakes and to park it appropriately? Of course not.

Well, by the same token, the purpose of life to expand in God's love should not be lost to you or reserved solely for meditative experiences. Hey, it's very easy to love all life when there's nobody else in the room, right? Experiment with holding thoughts of love toward others all the time and inwardly thank them for being a part of God's expanded love for you.

LOVE, KINDNESS AND MERCY, PART 1

While love, kindness and mercy has been fully discussed in other messages, what we wish to explain here is how the three are tied together. Indeed, many people discuss God's virtue qualities as if they are separated. The fact of the matter is that they are all mere attributes of the God Being state.

So, it is foolish for individuals to focus on each separately as if they exist apart from the whole. And, what is the whole? At one level the whole is expressed in that which some call Soul. At an even higher level it is that which is expressed as God. At an even higher level it is that which is known as Source. Its very nature is imperceptible to human awareness. Just as a drop of water from the ocean may not perceive the ocean in totality, so Soul, practically the highest expression of life for most human beings, may not perceive God or Source's totality. At best, just as the drop in the ocean may know its own qualities, so may the human being understand the qualities of God as it expresses itself in him.

The attributes of God include three fundamentals: knowing, being and creating. Knowing takes into account the capacity to be aware, to notice. The capacity of being takes into account the unitary expression of self, in that, in all truth, nothing exists and no-thing can exist. Creating takes into account the power of manifestation, this is to say, the ability to allow portions of itself to come into existence lacking full knowledge of themselves, others or even of it. Also, the capacity exists to instill within each aspect of itself sufficient loss, so that its very existence is conditioned by the strong desire to be completed. It is the eternal dance. So, the attribute of loving, kindness and mercy are but tenterhooks on the tree that is God, of itself.

Rather than pay attention to attributes and spend time making enormous effort to inculcate those into one's daily practice, does it not make more sense to master the art of merging one's Beingness with God and to acquire its vibrational sufficiency. There are a number of suggestions available that lend themselves to this experience as a greater possibility. The Buddhists speak of mindfulness and encourage their adherents to practice using the mind in specific ways that are intended to release the focus of the mind on worldly things leading to the experience of what they call the void.

Deepak Chopra teaches an exercise of finding the space between thoughts and allowing one's attention to rest on that. One practice emphasizes the use of mantras, but, quite often, the students do not understand that the power of the mantra lies not in the sound, but rather in the non-sound between the syllables. Indeed, the mantra establishes a vibrational frequency, but the attunement of the student to its resonances between the syllables establishes the access to the consciousness that is intended.

All life is a sequence of sounds, ranging from the lowest possible vibration reminiscent of a subwoofer all the way to that in the Source. Because vibration is a phenomenon associated with matter and density, it is oxymoronic to suppose that Source has vibration. Source is simply All and incorporates and creates that which vibrates. It does not.

LOVE, KINDNESS AND MERCY PART 2

Let us return to the question of the attributes of God and underscore the following point. To be sure, you may gain some sense of the godly virtues by examining them and trying your very best to express them, but the efforts, however, admirable they may be, will yield few results. To seek higher states in this way is not unlike a basketball player tugging at his shoe laces in hope that his efforts will increase his vertical leaping ability. The practice of spiritual exercises, meditations, and contemplation indeed grant an individual greater peace and harmony, truth and wisdom, which is an admirable pursuit.

But they do not bring people closer to the God state. At best, what they do is approximate aspects of the God state, which, if that is all that is available to them, is worthy.

What must be understood is that all of the spiritual practices are nothing but preparations for receiving and living with complete God awareness. This cannot be accomplished until Source awareness is installed by one in which it is already vested. While this process is somewhat similar to deekshas, Shakti Pats and initiations, it is not the same. Shakti Pats and initiations have transient effects. In both cases, they give recipients a sense of the Divine. This is not unlike the samples restaurants sometimes offer to passerby's in the hopes of luring recipients into the restaurants. After a very short time, just like the passerby who continues on, the recipients of these techniques revert to their prior state of consciousness.

Deekshas, on the other hand, are more permanent in their experience, granting recipients the full experience of God, with only one shortcoming. The individual's experience of God is locked into that state. The experience does not include within it the capacity to advance into higher states of consciousness. This is an ulterior, but not sinister intention. That is, that all are directly related to the master's spiritual mission, which, in most cases, requires devotees. To be sure, the followers amplify the master's capacity to achieve his spiritual mission on the planet, which is tied to the elevation of human consciousness. So it is absolutely necessary for the master to use whatever attunements, endowments or empowerments that he has to engage rather than ensnare the devotees with the accomplishment of his mission.

Because few paths engage in routine and intentional healing of their devotees, most of the ordinary human ego-based frailties manifest themselves, in petty power struggles, bitterness, arguments, and self-righteous judgments. These fall under the heading of "ashram politics." All of these are modulated by the individuals' proximity to the master and, sometimes, by individuals' ability to quote or cite the master's words and ideas. The master spends almost no time supporting the healing of the devotees and abandons them to their own follies, as long as they stay aligned with his mission. Only those close to the master, particularly those in line to succeed him, would have the advantage of personal healing support. The remaining devotees are simply left to their own devices. And, so it has been up to now.

With our decision to make Ascension widely available to humankind, the opportunity to express at once the full range of Divine virtues, to heal all aspects of human consciousness and to transform one's life into a fully Divine experience is now here. For this reason, the Light Givers program has **three essential stages**: the Universal Healer, which focuses on the elimination and healing of all attributes that obscure the realization of one's personal Divinity, the realization of personal Divinity, and the Ascension program that extends Divine awareness.

We install within all Universal Healer practitioners attunements that make available a range of experiences to recipients: **these include auric clearing and healing; soul clearing and healing; and the Ascensions**. There is one important stipulation: you do not have to believe in them to experience them. As long as you can accept and trust your own experience, you will know they have occurred. Once you have these experiences and know how to maintain them, there will be no doubt in your mind.

THE SPIRITUAL MIND – PART I

Most people accept the idea that a major purpose and challenge of life is that of being more godlike. To some this means making a list of things that must be done regularly. To others, this means holding specific thoughts as long as possible. And to others, this means being accountable and guilty when the foregoing are not accomplished. The flaw in each of these approaches is that individuals are relying on a tool that is ill-equipped for truly spiritual or Godly thought – the mind.

While many teachers speak of the lower mind and the higher mind with some degree of authority, they do not realize they are misleading their students. To be sure, the lower mind and the higher mind do exist, but they are part and parcel of the same cloth. The lower mind might focus on strong emotions, sex and anger. The higher mind, instead, focuses on love and beauty. The problem is that these are all mental activities and, by definition, are completely unrelated to spiritual realities. Where does Ascension fit?

Ascension, which simply re-centers one into a slightly higher reality, allows one to transcend mental activities and to experience what can only be called spiritual thinking. So, rather than seeing life as the result of interactions between and among people, things, events and so on, spiritual thinking is not really thinking at all. The process is more akin to noticing what is presenting itself and, most importantly, how it reflects the Beingness of God internally. How do you know when something reflects God's Beingness? Quite simply, it has to do with how you experience yourself because, after all, aren't you given to understand that you are, indeed, a spark of God, a God Being. So, in this state your perceptions are in relation to the resonance of your spiritual core.

The idea that you are a spark of God, Soul, a unit of awareness and so on is a fairly common belief. Surely, there is nothing unique about that. For most, it is simply a strongly held belief. The problem with the strength of the belief is that, for many, such a belief strongly held can interfere with the fundamental realization of your personal divinity. How? You never lose your freedom of choice. Your belief can overwhelm your experience of direct knowing to the point where you can fail to acknowledge or even respect the gift of direct knowing. So, you must choose to accept or see your spiritual experiences on a continuous basis. Ascension, to be sure, provides you directly with a being relocated to a world of higher experience, one that you must choose to accept.

Notice, you are being asked to accept your own higher experience. Some paths, at this point, ask you to accept a spiritual master as the purveyor of the higher reality. No, in fact, you yourself are the purveyor of the higher reality. For many, their acceptance of "the master" obligates them to a lifetime of what is tantamount to spiritual servitude. Your acceptance of the master should only be at the start. From that point, the master's grip should loosen. So, by the time you reach Soul awareness, the joys of spiritual freedom need be in your realization of the heavenly world and even greater experiences of God, as It presents itself to you, not a deepened dependence or neediness on your spiritual teacher for even higher initiations or the worrisome fear of losing those you already have. If anything, it should be a deepening independence as one further submerges into God's heart and of ever widening joy. How can one be spiritually free if he or she has to look to another personality for upliftment?

In truth, what makes a master, a master, is his or her understanding of the human and spiritual consciousness and his willingness to assist others to gain their understanding. Some are vested with the capacity to give energetic support, via Shakti Pats, Deekshas, transmissions and initiations. A few are gifted to support Ascension. And, some, in order to attract followers, chelas and students exhibit many clairvoyant skills and propagate channeled writings as evidence of their spiritual superiority and knowledge, further strengthening their hold on their followers. They either do not admit to their followers that they are little more than mouthpieces for disembodied entities or they let their followers assume their channeled information reflects some sort of spiritual advancement.

The sole purpose of the energetic support given is to help understand the spiritual mind and let free will and freedom of choice help guide one's awareness into the worlds of Being. Wherever personality projects itself, whether a master on a stage or a disembodied entity, resist words, thoughts or suggestions that imply the need to develop a more than temporary relationship. And, while they will admit that Holy Spirit takes on their form, they accept and publicize experiences with that form, as if it was them in conscious awareness. Of course, masters have different missions and there are obviously degrees of mastership and ways in which masters are charged to reveal themselves to the world. There is one and only one criterion of mastership - his or her spiritual purpose in service to whom he serves or wishes to serve.

THE SPIRITUAL MIND PART 2

In the Light Giver work, there are three Ascensions generally available: Soul, God and Source (these are presented at www.lightgivers.org). Anyone that goes beyond that is being trained to provide energetic support to others. The training may be completed on a weekend, a few months or longer, depending on the interest expressed. Dependence on anyone in this work is strongly discouraged. There is neither membership, recruitment or solicitation of dues- paying members. Information is available, but not required reading.

It is a conceit among humans that what they see, hear, and observe allows the accurate interpretation of life. This is so far from the truth. Ordinary thinking is based on reflections about the world that are couched in terms, ideas and experiences of worldly or earthly preoccupation. Elsewhere, we have called the mind an echo box. Spiritual thinking, on the other hand, is couched as It were, solely in reference to God, Spirit and Infinity. It is so far outside the box that the box is not even a reference point: thinking in terms of results, outcomes, effects, causes and so forth.

The spiritual thinker operates in a completely different realm. There, thought solely focuses and revolves around (revolve is as close to the nature of motionless that is present). Its sole reference is in relationship to God, Source, the Creator, the higher self or whatever higher expression the individual accepts as manifest. Can you see the distinction of levels of reality here? The focus of the human being is within the worlds of materiality and causality, which, by definition are limited. The human mind's attention is on the finite: the body, the emotion, the memory, the mind, and even the emergences from the subconscious.

So attention, which, by all rights should be vested directly upon higher realities, is split among concerns about one's body and its own mortality, the ravages of emotions, lost among the halls of memories, overwhelmed among the apprehensions and ruminations of the mind, and, finally, suborned by the underlayment of the subconscious mind. Rather than being the sole focus of one's attention, spiritual reality, at best, might show up during a morning or evening contemplation or even be as brief as a passing thought. What a pity!

Spiritual thought on the other hand, while noticing the passing realities of the mortal existence, loses itself among the higher dimensions and measures, as it were, life solely in relation to spirit. This point cannot be overemphasized and has been placed before humans in so many ways. Consider the lyrics of the spiritual, "Build your hopes on things eternal, hold to God's unchanging hand;" "Pray unceasingly;" "Chant the names of God;" and so on. It requires almost a Herculean effort to keep these thoughts before us. What is simply not understood is that it is practically impossible to do this. In fact, probably more thought is given to, "Whoops, what am I thinking about? I should be thinking these holy thoughts." How difficult this is. Ask yourselves, why is this so difficult? The simple fact is that you are attempting to accomplish spiritual thinking with your mental faculty, something that cannot be done. Even when you "think" you are doing it, you are not. Why? You are using your mind.

Spiritual thinking is a gift you receive via Ascension. When you are re-centered outside the worlds of cause and effect, you are given access to what can only be called your spiritual mind and that is the ability to see things in only one light, i.e., the extent to which what is noticed relates to the ultimate and higher truth of Oneness. Rather than seeing the world as one of cause and effect, you become aware of the exquisite opportunity you now have to see all life in relation to its Oneness.

What does this mean? It's actually quite simple. Instead of seeing life and the actions of others in relation to how it affects you, what it means to you, how they illustrate principles that you hold true, you find yourself noticing the ways in which all truly is of God and how each and every thing you see is in some way truly in its origin and intent and, in fact, an opportunity to experience, in one way or another, God's merciful, forgiving and loving heart. Now, this may make sense to you mentally and will remain a rumination of your thought process. If you have completed Sourccination, then you have an opportunity that few have. And, that is, ask your mind to release any thoughts it has about spiritual thinking. Why? Because as long as the mind is holding onto the concept of spiritual thinking, it blocks the process.

Allow your attention now to notice the clarity of your attention. The nature of spiritual thinking is quite different from that of the process of thought. Mental thinking moves on the waves of reflection, repetition and recollection. Spiritual thinking moves on the waves of Beingness. The extent to which you are submerged into spirit is the extent to which you will notice the spirituality of your own thought. This will show up truly in the levels of forgiveness you find yourself expressing.

There is a sense of freedom, openness, acceptance and all the divine virtues that spontaneously manifest. Rather than focusing on the dynamics of cause and effect in a personal way, your entire way of being is in relation to Spirit, God, the Creator and so forth. Be advised, the mind, threatened by your entry or re-centering outside of it in the higher reality, will make every effort to block your reliance upon the spiritual mind. This is a struggle that it cannot win because seeing the world with the eye of God is your spiritual destiny.

THE TRUE MEANING OF ASCENSION

It has come to our attention that the use of the term "Ascension" confuses some and confounds others. In this dictation, we wish to make clear exactly what is had in mind with this term and, more importantly, to help understand the spiritual significance of its availability. First, there are some rather common interpretations of the term. The most familiar is that association with Jesus' entry into the heavenly worlds in full consciousness and in the view of his disciples. So, what is conjured up with the word is something that Jesus went through and is, thereby, because he is the Son of God, and simply unavailable to us. Worse yet, we are not even candidates for such a process.

Other definitions of Ascension focus on different transformations. In some cases, it involves the transformation of the physical body following a very long and detailed process of cleansing, contemplating, energizing, etc. In some systems, the process involves actually experiencing, albeit briefly, physical death. While these are worthy processes to which few aspire and even fewer succeed, our focus on Ascension is concerned with the transformation of consciousness. In some venues the transformation is considered a movement of a sort, i.e. Soul Travel. In other venues, it is spoken of as relocation and awakening. Even in our own writings, whether intended or not, there is an implication of travel. Indeed, the root word of ascend, is the Latin ascendere, which means "to climb."

Let us be clear here. There is no climbing. There is no movement. There is neither traveling nor relocating. Closest to the actual experience of ascension is the notion of awakening. Imagine if you will a huge living tapestry with only a limited awareness. Say, for example, the tapestry is one million square miles. But, even though it's alive, it is only aware of one square inch. There is no movement of consciousness with the tapestry. There is simply the limited consciousness. As the tapestry becomes more aware of itself, would you say it's moving? Of course not, it is simply awakening to itself, which is already here and there. There, illusion of movement is given by the recognition of awareness elsewhere.

If we ask you to put your attention on your hand and then to shift your attention to your foot, will anything move? Awareness of different places involves no movement. There is only the awareness of the separateness of the realizations. Imagine, if you will, becoming completely aware, as the tapestry, of its entirety. Does this mean that the awakened aspect of the tapestry will necessarily behave differently. Not necessarily. To the extent that the tapestry understands that it exists solely to exist, each awakened aspect may eventually come to realize that its sole purpose is to be a part of the tapestry that demonstrates its union with the whole.

By the same token, we each are living parts of the tapestry of Source. Ascension, as such, does not yield to mental understanding, comprehension or mastery. Ascension is best understood by going through the process, i.e., accepting the possibility, undergoing the healings and clearing, and noticing the expansions and shifts in awareness and the transformation of temporal reality to a focus on direct experience and the truth that is Now, in this moment, nowhere else but here! Once you experience it, you know!

FORGIVENESS VS. ABSOLUTION

Forgiveness is thought by many to be almost a supreme act of humanity. Forgiveness was Jesus' final act before he died. Forgiveness, i.e. the willingness to ignore or overlook an offense, is truly human in that we take into account some aspect of behavior. So, when we forgive, it is with the recognition that an offense has occurred and is lodged in our memory. Something has happened, which presumably affected us and though it remains lodged in our memories and energies, we originate feelings of neutrality that retard the effect felt previously of some action and consciously forgive the individual that committed the offense.

So, with forgiveness, we act and function as if the forgivable act did not occur. Yet, unconsciously the perpetrator is on notice that the forgivable act ought not occur again, lest forgiveness not be offered as easily. In a sense, forgiveness is a malleable event, in that it has some variance, which is to say that there are dimensions of the forgivable act that may exceed the forgiver's capacity. For example, if an individual is found to have stolen an item for a local store, how likely is he to be forgiven if he returns to the store and appropriates yet another item. If a sister borrows an article of clothing from a sibling without permission, how likely is that sibling to forgive a repeated transgression? So, implicit in forgiveness, there is a sense of limitation. There is also a great sense of choice in that the forgiver is not bound to forgive the transgressor.

But absolution is wholly different.

While individuals are vested with the capacity to forgive others, the power of absolution is not within the grasp of humanity. For absolution is divinely ordained Forgiveness occurring within the veil of memory and with the scope of things done, acted upon and reacted to. But absolution erases the record. Not only is there no memory of it; it is as if it never occurred. Why is this important to understand? It is because we each have the power of creation with our thoughts and deeds. But, do we have the power of absolution?

Absolution is a purely Divine Attribute, something that only God can grant, but it may be delegated or given as a dispensation by God to those doing His work. In most cases, where it does occur, the phrase, "In Jesus' Name," precedes the absolution. And, in what form does the absolution occur? It occurs in the form of the forgiveness of sin. But Divine forgiveness is far greater than human forgiveness. Human forgiveness requires the acknowledgement that a practically unforgiveable act has occurred. The acknowledgement is by both the forgiver and the forgiven. The act, whatever it was, remains a stain on the relationship, much as a stain might be present, although invisible to others, on a garment. Others may not see it, but the wearer of the garment remains aware of where the stain was located. But the same token, the forgiven act remains ever present.

Absolution is implied by the scripture Psalm 51: 18 King James Bible

"Purge ME with hyssop, and I shall be clean: wash me, and I shall be whiter than snow. "So, absolution is more of a total and complete act than the mere act of forgiveness at the human level. Absolution completely dissolves not only the sinful act, but sin itself as a component of the individual's awareness. Completely absolved, not only is the memory of sin wiped from your recall, but the Divine Act removes it from your Being, in that instant.

Now, here is the rub. There is no spiritual "Scotchgard" that prevents one from reacquiring sin, restraining their spiritual cloth, and, if sin is the precursor to damnation, there is nothing to prevent the individual for re-entering the path of damnation. In order words, while absolution makes possible the entry into the heavenly state of personal divinity, it is no guarantee. Thus, in the moment that you are Divinely absolved, you are only at the brink of personal divinity, where you may teeter back into the pre-absolution stage or you may plunge ahead into your personal divinity. The choice is yours.

So, how do you make the plunge? Here's something to ponder. Jesus Christ was the acknowledged "Son of God," working miracle after miracle: giving sight to the blind, helping the lame to walk, and recalling to life the dead. Yet it is seldom remarked about how much he prayed. Read the New Testament and note the many times that he is described as having been in prayer. Particularly interesting is how he responded to his disciples when they complained about their inability to cast out a particular spirit. Jesus told them that, in order to be able to do what he does, prayer and fasting were required. You have to assume that Jesus lived in a completely absolved state of Being and was completely free of sin. Yet he prayed much.

Paul, in his epistle to the Thessalonians, wrote:

17 Pray without ceasing. 18 In everything give thanks: for this is the will of God in Christ Jesus concerning you. 19 Quench not the Spirit. 20 Despise not prophesying. 21 Prove all things; hold fast that which is good. 22 Abstain from all appearance of evil. 23 And the very God of peace sanctify you wholly; and I pray God your whole spirit and soul and body be preserved blameless unto the coming of our Lord Jesus Christ. 1 Thessalonians 5:17-27 (King James Version)

To maintain his permanently absolved state of being, Jesus continuously reminded listeners of His relationship with the heavenly Father:

John 5:19 Then answered Jesus and said unto them, Verily, verily, I say unto you, The Son can do nothing of himself, but what he seeth the Father do: for what things soever he doeth, these also doeth the Son likewise.

John 5:30 I can of mine own self do nothing: as I hear, I judge: and MY judgment is just; because I seek not mine own will, but the will of the Father which hath sent me.

John 8:28 Then said Jesus unto them, When ye have lifted up the Son of man, then shall ye know that I am he, and that I do nothing of MY self; but as MY Father hath taught me, I speak these things.

John 8:29 And he that sent ME is with me: The Father hath not left ME alone; for I do always those things that please him.

Jesus presented himself as the Son of God and eschewed the idea that the work he did was somehow independent, telling those with whom he met that God was acting through him. And, he spent a good deal of time in prayer, which affirms the necessity, no matter how sinless or absolved one might be, of being constantly in prayer and/or meditating upon the Divine.

So those that wish to maintain their state of absolution or freedom from karma should remain aware that while they are completely free in the moment, a certain diligence is required to maintain their freedom: in particular, diligent attention to God that can be experienced internally, as contrasted to the illusions of life that are experienced externally.

THE TRUE MEANING OF WORSHIP

In this dictation we will explain the true meaning of worship. The Bible is replete with examples of what God did to those who did not put Him first. While it is clear that such compliance was necessary for the Israelites' survival in the face of their enemies, the question to be considered for the modern man is the extent to which such allegiance is required today. Well, quite frankly, it is not important to many, if you take a look at what they regard as being mainly important in their lives: possessions, relationships and for some, drugs, money, sex and alcohol.

Maintaining God's primacy today is best understood as being required of those that seek to enter and maintain a heavenly state of awareness. In other words, those that wish to live in the Kingdom of God while still on planet earth. In this context, this would be those that wish, not only to experience Sourccination and Ascension, but who desire to live as Ascended beings while still physically embodied in this reality. Do not misunderstand us, the entire Sourccination and Ascension process was brought out, so that they who have not come into a true awareness or understanding of what lies behind traditional religion may access their spiritual goals without surrendering their spiritual freedom to the false teachers, preachers and pastors.

It is well recognized that many of those that parrot Biblical sayings and parables are spiritually bankrupt. Many have enriched themselves and been found to be not only financially immoral, but to have committed immoral sexual acts. In many cases, however, the hunger of their followers for the Kingdom of God has been so great, that not only were they forgiven by their flocks, but their followers continued to look to them for spiritual guidance. To our way of thinking, if someone so immersed in God's work proved to be so morally and financially bankrupt, sinning at the levels that many have, it would warrant calling into question, not only them, but also the religious path that they follow and would warrant seeking another leader.

Within the concept of worship, there is an implicit self-identification. This means that true worship, in some way, binds the worshipper to that which is worshipped. When Moses came down from the mountain with the Ten Commandments in tablet form, he was astonished to see that, in his absence, the children of Israel had erected monuments to other Gods and had breached, in a way, their relationship with God. In other words, rather than taking the time that Moses was away to cement their relationship with the God of their fathers, they abandoned He who had parted the Red Sea and was leading them and feeding them in the wilderness. They were no longer bound, in their minds, to the God of their forefathers. What they did not understand, as so many do not today, is that the singular purpose of the human existence is to so completely identify with God or Source that one is unable inwardly to distinguish the two.

This is a difficult concept to understand. Mentally, it makes no sense. Why? Because the truth it shares is incomprehensible. The logic upon which it is based is spiritual logic that can only be experienced, which is at the heart of worship. Spiritual logic bases itself upon the wisdom gained through Ascension, which is an ever-widening pool of expanding knowledge. Things that make sense tend to be linear, depending upon logical and systematic thinking.

Correct worship requires surrender, detachment, self-denial, acceptance of absolution, recognition of ascension and, most importantly, willingness to be completely absorbed by Spirit, the Holy God, the ECK or whatever name is assigned to it. If the question is asked, "How is this different from meditation?" The answer is that, there is no difference if the object of meditation is God, Source or the Allness in Allness. Of course, there are some meditators who would argue that meditation should be accomplished by having no object of meditation, only the act itself. To which we will respond by saying, that remains to be seen.

Again, Jesus provides a wonderful example of how he maintained his state of worship by keeping the focus of all his words and deeds on God. He kept his divine relationship before them:

John 5:19 Then answered Jesus and said unto them, Verily, verily, I say unto you, The Son can do nothing of himself, but what he seeth the Father do: for what things soever he doeth, these also doeth the Son likewise.

John 5:30 I can of mine own self do nothing: as I hear, I judge: and MY judgment is just; because I seek not mine own will, but the will of the Father which hath sent me.

John 8:28 Then said Jesus unto them, When ye have lifted up the Son of man, then shall ye know that I am he, and that I do nothing of MY self; but as MY Father hath taught me, I speak these things.

John 8:29 And he that sent ME is with me: The Father hath not left ME alone; for I do always those things that please him.

We suggest you spend time maintaining your divine relationship daily, both in contemplation and in waking daily life, being aware that you and the Divine are inseparable.

Many Blessings,
The Light Givers

LOVE AND THE ABILITY TO ACHIEVE YOUR LIFE MISSION AND DESTINY

ASCENDED MASTER TREMULEN

What is seldom understood in the study of the spiritual and healing works and, indeed, that which is often overlooked, is the importance of the spiritual vibration of the heart and the love for Source as key to moving through the gates of the astral, causal, mental, etheric and soul plane to Source. While the astral plane is the location and source of love for many, unless the feeling of love is harmonized and resonant with an overwhelming love of Source and its works, the transition through the astral plane is unlikely. This is because of the many attachments that accompany the phenomenon of such love as experienced by many. Such love becomes personalized and individualized to persons, places and things for how they, in some way, represent some integral aspect that is important to the individual.

Similarly, the love that manifests solely on the causal plane has its own separate and separating character. The individual, imbued with such love, places great value on history, on what has been experienced, on the future and what will be experienced, and feels great affinity for such. Often these individuals are history buffs and planners. Yet, they risk the challenges faced by those who are stuck in the love dimensions of the other planes. Unless there is the strong aspect of Source love, there is little likelihood of moving to higher planes and broader visions. There is a possessive element of such love that is strong. It has almost a material aspect.

It has been generally recognized down through the ages that the great spiritual masters and beings have been strongly imbued with Source, but what has been seldom understood is that such was not accidentally bestowed upon them. Indeed, such came about because of their awareness, not their intention to magnify the loving presence of Source in their life through magnifying their love for others.

No better example of such is Brother Lawrence, who, on a daily basis, practiced – note the word *practiced* – the presence of Source in his life. Similarly, love must be practiced on a daily basis at every opportunity. This does not mean going around saying to everyone, "I love you." What it does mean is letting the feeling of love, which we all know, permeate every single aspect of our being. Just think about it. You can achieve the highest conscious awareness available by practicing the art of loving, and, believe me, many, many opportunities for such come almost at every moment, even moments of which you are unaware. When your eyes open in the morning, rather than groaning and moaning, greet the new day with a feeling of love. Turn to your mate, your pet, your morning newspaper, with love. Practice the feeling of love. Just think, you now have the Secret of the Ages and the Key to the Source – the feeling of love.

Now, this does not mean that you will not have emotional reactions. Of course, you will. You are human. And this does not mean that you will not have unloving moments. Of course, you will. But it does mean that, on balance, your practice will pay off and you will enter the Source in a full loving consciousness.

The most important step that you took or will take in your journey to the Source worlds is the Light Giver Ascensions. Why? Because for many, that decision is an acknowledgement that the Light Giver Ascensions, empowerments and healings will transform the individual into Source. For many, it is recognition that their core identity is that of Soul, that they are finite parts of the infinite. They are engaged on a path of continuous evolution that may be directly influenced by them. They are now free of the vagaries of fate, the whims of chance, and the uncertainties of a life built upon contingencies. They are now fully cognizant of the fact that they are embarked on a glorious journey of mastery, a true sailor of the cosmos, and, indeed, a master of their own fates. Thus, the Soul Ascension essentially gathers the Light Giver up and propels him or her forward on a journey, for certain, to Godhood, with a loving heart as the passport to Source.

The difference between the Source-Ascended person and the Soul-Ascended person is that the Soul-Ascended person now knows that the life he or she lives, or has lived, is clearly the result of the choices that have been made over the course of many lifetimes. The Source-Realized person knows that the choices that will be made throughout the remainder of his or her existence will always be informed by what is for the greatest good. In the first example, the affinity of the decisions was retrospective always, either for the specific interest of a person, a thing or group or, most often, for the individual. But it is backwards looking. In the second example, the decision is in the here and now, made for the whole, and, if anything, forward looking, albeit in the moment.

Imagine, if you will, looking at one's multiple lifetimes as if looking through many prisms and kaleidoscopes. One will see that Soul in its movement through each is in a continuous process of transformation and that, along the way, Soul's mission for each lifetime is recalibrated to help achieve its ultimate goal, Source Ascension, in terms of complete affinity with the Divine mission. It should be pointed out that the movement is not linear. Soul, in its efficiency, will send various aspects of itself through multiple, parallel, and coincident incarnations. Thus, it is not impossible for the individual to meet other aspects of the self and not only resolve the karma of the specific path of evolution but also the karma of coincident evolution. So, the individual aspect of Soul, in meeting another aspect of itself, will feel as if they are destined to relate in some way and as if fate has brought them together. While fatalism determinism is not an operating reality, in terms of the interplay of free will and the eventual outcome, there is the opportunity to resolve some karmic circumstances and to facilitate the rapid evolution of both Soul aspects.

Now, while this seems to support the idea of the old Soul Mate theory, such is not the case. It is wholly possible, in most instances, that the interplay between two people who have such feelings is, in fact, the interplay between like karmic resonances and that what must be done is to learn how to harmonize the dissonances, rather than the counter-productivity of constructing lifelong agreements. This gives even further justification to the necessity of one's focus remaining solidly on Source Realization and on solidifying and stabilizing one's consciousness within that Domain.

In this lesson, a great amount of information has been shared, information that has been deliberately constructed to help open your heart and to align you more fully with Source, and, in so doing, the Source that is within you manifests as the Source that is you, and you become and are the light that illuminates and heals the world, greeting all whom you meet as the embodiment of Source.

Gregory

THE STAGES OF LOVE

ASCENDED MASTER REBAZAR TARZ

The Ascension Master's immersion in the field of love and, indeed, the facility of love as the tool to advance spiritually has only just begun. In fact, what the experience of love becomes as the Ascension Master advances on the path toward, into, and beyond God-Realization bears faint resemblance to how love is experienced in the early stages. While the love experienced by most humans is powerful and uplifting, it is like the finger pointing at the moon, in that, while the finger shows you the moon, it is not the moon itself. It is fairly easy to exhort, cajole and persuade you that love is important, but it is quite another thing to teach you how to magnify and exemplify it in your daily life.

In the next few sentences, I will give you the keys to love. First, everyone is imbued with a glimmer of what love is, who to love, and where to love. That is a fact. For some, it is a person, a memory, a place, an event, an act, and so on. The feeling of love is there, and what is that feeling? It is a feeling of completion, a feeling of selflessness, a feeling of transference. But what is common is a feeling of in some way being in touch with something that is greater than oneself. Can you see, therefore, how love anticipates the experience of Source?

Let us go on. Second, there is the act of love. It involves conscious choice, that is to say, that it always involves choices. Now, there are some who will say, no, love is automatic, it just happens. While that may seem like what has been experienced, in all truth, if the moment of loving is experienced in slow motion, the individual would realize that every single time there was an instant when the choice was made to love. This then is the foundation and key to the expansion of love in the Ascension Master's heart: choosing to love. This choice must be made and diligently applied. I cannot emphasize this enough. He or she who wishes to enter Source Realization must consistently make the Source-inspired choice. It can be no less than this. In this way, love, which is the complete underpinning of existence, will find great harmony and resonance in the Ascension Master's heart and become a magnifying force and cause for all actions, making not only a stronger link between free will and Divine will, but eventually allowing the movement of Divine Will to be the impulse for all actions.

In Source, what becomes extraordinarily clear is the feeling of Oneness, often so rhapsodized in various places. But love in action means nothing without the capacity to move in harmony with other Source Beings. He or she who sings the praises of being One with All but who acts continuously as an adversary or lives in conflict has yet to completely understand what Oneness truly means. So, with the realization of the necessity of Oneness to gain the God-love or bliss state, there needs to be the inner release of those attitudes, memories or feelings that bind the Ascension Master to a lower state. The view that must be held is that Source is pulling the individual Soul to its heart as a mighty force. At the same time, the Ascension Master has barriers and holds on him or her that are resisting Source's call and preventing the easy movement of the Ascension Master to God's heart, preventing the expansion of love in the heart, and thus hindering the acquisition of the Source knowledge. There are many things that you will do in your life. Much will be achieved, but do not be mistaken, this is your purpose and destiny, to achieve Source knowledge, Source Realization and beyond.

In this lesson, a great amount of information has been shared, information that has been deliberately constructed to help open your heart and to align you more fully with Source, and, in so doing, the Source that is within you manifests as the Source that is you, and you become and are the light that illuminates and heals the world, greeting all whom you meet as the embodiment of Source.

Gregory

FREE WILL AND DIVINE WILL

ASCENDED MASTER GOPAL DAS

The distinction between free will and Divine Will, as mentioned earlier, is seldom understood but is worthy of attention. To fully understand this, one must listen completely with the heart, but herein lays the secret of all spiritual teachings and is the key to ultimate mastery of the human consciousness. The greatest gift that the human has been given is the gift of free will. This is what has been used to explore the planet, to develop great inventions, and, indeed, to transcend the atmosphere. But it is all for naught if the free will of the human is not overlaid or replaced with the essence of Divine Will. The essence of free will is that of choice. The essence of Divine Will is, simply put, the basis of choice. Let ME make it clear. Free will begins and ends with choice. Divine Will is the anchor upon which the choice is made. Thus, in the exercise of free will, there are motives, reasons, purposes and such, all of which assign to the action a cause related to the perceived benefits that will be derived.

Divine Will does not work that way. It is like the tide that raises all boats; it operates for the good of all concerned without giving primary regard to the actor or originator of the choice. Certainly, the individual who acts or serves the Divine Will does so thoughtfully but quite freely. If you asked how free will might be developed to follow the Divine Will of Source, I would reply, "The answer is simple but complex, easy but hard, uncomplicated but complex." Why would I say this? Because she or he who approaches the question with firm intention is bound to fail. Whoever goes after the solution with a clear plan can be overcome by the challenge. If his decision is solely informed by free will, he will not only face insurmountable odds, but he is doomed to fail. It is the difference between the anxiousness of chipping away at a block of ice to get fresh water or allowing it to melt, between sucking water through a pinhole in the top of container or simply removing the container lid and pouring the contents into another container.

What I am explaining here has been described, for lack of a better term, as Vairag, or detachment. It could also be described as being lovingly present, non-controlling, watchfully patient, lovingly disengaged, and a variety of other descriptions. The essential point is all centered on the idea and experience of taking actions in life with a viewpoint of freedom and kindness for all concerned, rather than just the self. Do I make MY point clear? With Divine Will comes an inner recognition of what is in harmony with all life. This does not mean there will not be differences based on personalities, perceptions and personal styles. This is normal. But underneath those differences, there is the solid awareness of what must be done to preserve and advance the harmony of all life, and it is humbling to know that this may be achieved simply by the practice of love. It is also humbling to know that without the practice and accomplishment of such, the heavenly worlds may not be entered.

Now, Vairag has an essential challenge, and, that is, in all applications it translates as, "detachment from," when, in truth, the dynamic is one of absorption in, which is to say that becoming Source Realization is not the result of moving from a state, but it is the transformation into a state. It is like the choice a child makes when it truly chooses the ice cream flavor he or she wants. Does the child stand before the counter bemoaning the fact that it won't taste all the flavors of the ice cream that he or she did not choose? Of course not. The child stands there completely absorbed in anticipation of the flavor that it has chosen. In his or her mind's eye, he or she sees the cone, the glistening and softly melting ice cream, feels the creamy texture and tastes the chosen flavor on the tongue. So is being Source. While to an observer they appear detached, in reality, they are completely absorbed, if I mix the metaphor in the flavor of God. Mark those words, the flavor of God, which is Divine love.

In this lesson, a great amount of information has been shared, information that has been deliberately constructed to help open your heart and to align you more fully with Source, and, in so doing, the Source that is within you manifests as the Source that is you, and you become and are the light that illuminates and heals the world, greeting all whom you meet as the embodiment of Source.

Gregory

TREMBLING AT THE GATES OF HEAVEN

ASCENDED MASTER REBAZAR TARZ

There are many who spend their entire lifetimes trembling at the gates of the heavenly worlds, fearful that they are unworthy of admission, poring over books, texts, and even discourses such as these, hoping that one more word, one more concept, one more class, indeed, one more initiation, will gain them admission. What folly! There are planes and levels of consciousness far beyond the gates of the Source worlds, and those who do not gain entry do so not because they are unworthy but because they have accepted the foolishness of holy men, gurus and others who make the heavenly worlds appear unreachable.

Heaven is here now and firmly within your grasp. You must diligently apply what we are teaching you so that not only will you enter the heavenly worlds and gain the consciousness of Source, you will take up greater spiritual and healing responsibilities in the physical and inner worlds and help those who assist Source to carry out its Divine tasks. What you must understand is that your very reading of these words is an acknowledgement of the many lifetimes of spiritual development and evolution that you have experienced and of your readiness for spiritual and healing mastery. You are not an Ascension Master to be a perpetual spiritual and healing student; you are to become a Master. Indeed, some of you are becoming a master – yet again.

Your confidence in your spiritual and healing power was so great that you could comfortably accept the spiritual amnesia of rebirth, knowing that you would be again connected with Source and transformed to an even higher level of Beingness. It is this certainty that has propelled your spiritual search, and it is this certainty that has brought you to this point. The gates of Source are universally open to individuals of all walks of life; and its obtainment is reliant on the individual's soul development and spiritual training of other lifetimes.

We do not mean to assign all the responsibility to you for developing yourself spiritually. You cannot do it alone, despite all the things that let you know that the Master's job is to help get you to the Soul Plane and the Self-Realized state, and it is said that from that point you go on to Source, as if by yourself. You do not go by yourself. You cannot go by yourself. It would be a contradiction to say that. In the Source-Realized state, you must cooperate with other Source Beings, but you must gain that level of consciousness without the support and direct involvement of your spiritual teachers. What does happen is that your relationship with the Master changes. You go from being a highly-dependent Ascension Master, like a child on a bicycle with training wheels, to one who is pedaling ahead with a parent jogging alongside. The parent only reaches to help when such help is absolutely needed. The parent gives gentle instruction, is available to answer questions, mainly operates in silence, but is watchful all the time.

It is Gregory's job to model the relationship that you will have when you enter the Source and to help support your transition from free will to Divine Will in full knowledge that the outcome of an action is less important than the state of consciousness of the action. Am I making sense?

Let ME go on. It is not enough to accept the goal of Source without fully committing to it. It is a goal that you will want to take fully into your very being, to make it a part of your very essence, nay, to make it your very essence, for to achieve it will bring rewards that you only thought existed in books written by holy men and women or in your imagination. You will experience yourself filled with light, love, and all the Divine virtues for which you have prayed these many years. Yet what makes the experience so exquisite is that the Source Ascension, while of foremost importance in your life, provides the background, underpinnings, musical score and melody; you remain the lyrics, but Source Realization enhances how you are living.

In this lesson, a great amount of information has been shared, information that has been deliberately constructed to help open your heart and to align you more fully with Source, and, in so doing, the Source that is within you manifests as the Source that is you, and you become and are the light that illuminates and heals the world, greeting all whom you meet as the embodiment of Source.

Gregory

FACING LIFE'S CHALLENGES

ASCENDED MASTER ST. FRANCIS OF ASSISI

In MY life, as in yours, there were many challenges. By no means do we wish to minimize the difficulties that you face in daily living. For some, in these times, just keeping food on the table, fuel in the vehicle and clothes on one's back may seem purely insurmountable. It is so easy to say that Source loves you or this is part of your spiritual development, and, while I will admit that I do believe that, accepting that way of being cannot be based solely on what someone else says. You must, as an individual, be open to the possibility that this is true, that your life really is a gift from Source and that love, like the spark that begins the forest fire, can become such a raging inferno in your heart, that nothing, and I do mean nothing can stand against it.

This is how it was for me. As I faced soldiers of MY king, distrustful parishioners and fellow men of the cloth, it was truly MY faith, belief and certainty of God's love and protection that guided ME There are some who say that you must live "as if." I say you must live "as," in a level of pure certainty. Through MY daily practices, contemplations and keeping of MY full attention on love, God's love, and love for all others, I came to understand and see that nothing really mattered except mastering the art of living from the heart of God's love. With that focus came the blessings of heaven, and the kingdom of heaven opened to me. Thus, MY love for Source sustained MY life against all odds and eventually opened the Gates of Heaven and the Upper Source worlds.

In the Catholic Church, during MY day, there were many stresses and strains. Priests fought against priests, royalty and against royalty, and parishioners against parishioners. The tumult and divisiveness was spiritually deafening. Yet I, in MY own humble way, sought valiantly to remain above the fray. When I avoided going to meetings or responding to requests for involvement, I was accused of being distant. When I attended meetings or responded to inquiries, as the Divine Will led me, I was accused of being self-righteous. When I urged MY peers and colleagues to act and live according to their faith, I was called judgmental. For me, it was a time of great sadness to see that MY church had essentially lost its view of itself. In looking back on that time, I now see that by maintaining MY adherence to the basic tenets of MY faith and by being an example of love for Source and all life, it might be said that many of MY fellow churchmen were uplifted and recalled and recommitted to their own spiritual underpinnings. It was MY love for Source and for humanity that inspired MY life and which served to keep the Catholic Church from declining into self-destruction.

I share this message with you because you may find yourself faced with somewhat similar challenges in your own life and yet find ways in which to magnify God's love for yourself and others. You may find yourself in moments of quiet despair and aloneness. Do not fear, the life that you have constructed for yourself has such moments, as did the life that I constructed for MY self. Practice being in God's presence on a regular basis, if only for a few moments a day. Gradually expand the time and your attention. Practice the love of God. Be the love of God. This is your Divine purpose. This is your Divine Mission. The Gates of Heaven are open to all, for all.

The importance of the state of consciousness of an action, discussed earlier by Rebazar, cannot be overemphasized. Those who reach Self-Realization come to understand those thoughts or ways of being over which there is no control and make plans and commitments to align their lives more closely with the Divine Will. In so doing, they take the enabling power away from those thought forms and begin to disable their influence over choice. For some this will feel like a struggle and that it will be, for these forms have lives of their own. So it is only natural for them to struggle for their existence.

In this lesson, a great amount of information has been shared, information that has been deliberately constructed to help open your heart and to align you more fully with Source, and, in so doing, the Source that is within you manifests as the Source that is you, and you become and are the light that illuminates and heals the world, greeting all whom you meet as the embodiment of Source.

Gregory

LOVE AND DETACHMENT

ASCENDED MASTER KADMON

When this Universe was created and Soul was embedded into the lower worlds, the decision was reached that the heart would be the connecting point between the lower bodies and the heavenly world. But the individual Soul would have to learn the art, through what we know as love, of making the connection and expanding it to the level necessary for the individual to re-enter the Gates of Heaven. Thus, the use of techniques that lead to detachment, greater love and so forth, are all related to this fact, the heart is the beginning point of any true inquiry into God's Secrets of Life.

To work with this idea, the individual must learn to set aside the firm grip held upon by his or her mind, physical, emotion or memory experiences. Instead, the subtle art of shifting attention from truth to truth must be done in full alignment with the heart, so that as realizations come into manifestation, the individual's heart may expand, as will his realizations of his or her own Godhood. If the heart is undeveloped, in a spiritual sense, the individual will continue to recycle through the lower worlds until such development occurs.

Love is the key and is what must be practiced. There is a steadfastness of focus, a disciplined approach genuinely exercised that animates one's action. The motivating and animating force that creates, develops and sustains all universes can only be understood in the human consciousness of Love. But in the creation of universes, it is experienced as a much higher form. Nevertheless, there is a glimmer in the joy the parent first feels at the sight of a newborn, the happiness of a child at the sight of new fallen snow, the upliftment a newlywed gets when sighting his or her beloved and so on. This is the perpetual state of the Source Realized, at the core of their being, and is the state that simmers in your own heart, waiting to bubble over and out into your life. And this is the true state of awareness and being that brings all life into manifestation, which sustains it, and which helps it move even more so into a state of pure transcendence.

While life is best understood as being in the continuous now, it can also be understood as a sequence of interlocking momentary nows, while indistinguishable because of their interlocking nature can, at one level, be understood as subsequent seamless acts of love. In this light, a driver arriving home may see his or her commute, which consisted of many driving maneuvers around many automobiles, as a unitary phenomenon, "awful." The same driver may, likewise, having had the same drive, may say, "not bad," and be overwhelmed by feelings of love and appreciation for the comparable struggles of his compatriots on the road and the strong hope that they were able to reach their destinations safely. Indeed, each maneuver on the highway, each face looked into, each automobile seen, could have evoked a feeling of profound love and appreciation. To extend this point, driving requires a great deal of care and consideration of all drivers for each other, and, of course, for themselves. It is a great collaborative venture, one with excellent opportunities to practice love and actions for the good of the whole. The actions that anticipate Source Realization help to bring Source Realization into manifestation. Is this point clear?

In this lesson, a great amount of information has been shared, information that has been deliberately constructed to help open your heart and to align you more fully with Source, and, in so doing, the Source that is within you manifests as the Source that is you, and you become and are the light that illuminates and heals the world, greeting all whom meet you as the embodiment of Source.

Gregory

LIVING IN SOURCE

ASCENDED MASTER YAUBL SACABI

A central question of the Ascension Master is that of how to experience the joy and ecstasy of Source Beingness in every waking moment of their life. This is a question which has plagued holy men and women, healers and their students down through the ages. What can one do to ensure that Source fills one's complete essence? How can one's total consciousness be completely absorbed in God? It is the central focus that is exemplified in the statement by Krishna, who had throat cancer, when asked why did he not heal himself. He answered that he did not want to remove his attention from God. We teach the art of simultaneous awareness, so that, if it is consistent with your life contract, you may keep your attention on Source and heal your throat cancer.

Much is made in some teachings and by other writers of "Soul Travel." Some even speak of Soul Journey. Paul Twitchell even once called it bi-location. In each instance, what is being described, albeit inexactly, is not just the art of shifting one's attention or being in a state of continuous ecstasy. These are means to the end in the development of this art. The point of emphasis is on maintaining the center of one's beingness in the heart of Source by managing other activities simultaneously.

Now, the point which is often made by many teachers is that we or you are already operating at many levels, but, like a radio that has no tuner, you are unable, in most cases, to tune your personal frequency in such a way to see and know what is happening at most of those levels. In the human consciousness, no one can handle the volume of knowledge and information that is available. There are probably many in the higher worlds that could handle or would want to handle the volume of information being generated. So, there is a narrowing that occurs as a function of purpose, mission and alignment. Yet the basic frequency, much like the carrier wave for FM radio, is Divine love, and you are already filled with that carrier wave. Our purpose is to help you realize it by urging you to take whatever steps are necessary.

There are three elements that should be given attention. These accompany the awareness of Self as Soul. They are Seeing, Knowing and Being. While they are joined when experienced, we will discuss Beingness as a separate topic. Seeing, of course, is the art of looking deeply into a thing, a thought, an act, and so forth, as the ability to determine its apparent truth. We say apparent, because the truth is not completely known, without gaining the perspective of other Source-Realized Beings. Thus, while we may be able to distinguish between Relative Truth and Absolute Truth, no Source Being holds to a perspective without learning the perspectives and views of other Source Beings. This then helps explains the core necessity of doing all things for the good of the whole, in that it is early training in being aligned to the core essence and truths as others see it. Reality is jointly constructed. It does not exist outside or inside; it exists conjointly. Do I make MY self clear on this point?

In connection with this, then comes Knowing. This is the absolute certainly that one has at the moment of truth. It derives from the power of Seeing. It is the capability, at any moment, to recognize simultaneously the truth that presents itself to the Seer, and to recognize that the truth is incomplete without incorporating that which is seen by other Source Beings. This is important. In Knowing, there is Unknowing; in Seeing, there is Unseeing. This is the reality of all sentient beings.

Now, let us return to the question of Beingness. For some, this question is approached as if it is something that can be achieved from the inside out. So, they fill themselves with Source energy and, like a balloon, imagine that they can puff themselves up until, at last, they have achieved the Beingness of Source.

I will teach you yet another secret. What keeps the Beingness of Source from you is not what you are filled with or not filled with; it is your sense of separateness from all life. Drop the barriers between you and that which surrounds you. Let go of your inner attachments. Release your strong intentions and connections to the things that bind you to the lower worlds. You are filled with Beingness already. You just have to realize it and you will. You are already free. Let go of the chains.

To extend the metaphor, the human is like the fruit flies trapped in a bottle with a lid on it. After some time, the lid can be removed, yet the fruit flies will go no farther than where the lid was. But there is no lid. The limitation is in the expectations of the flies. Your limitations are in your expectations of yourself. There is no lid. You are not just human. You are a Source man or woman. There is no lid.

Paul Twitchell once wrote, "It is God who works and not you." This is both true and not true. To the end that you are operating from your lower self and self-motivation actions, Source actions are separate and distinct. Yet when you make a Source-inspired choice, whether or not you are self-motivated, if Source is on the field, then the Divine force will predominate. The point that is illustrated here is the power of intention, the idea being that the single intention that the Source Being must have is simply that.

There is the old story of the chela that asked his teacher what must he do to have God, in this case, God Realization. The teacher marched the student into a nearby river and asked the seeker to put his head beneath the river's surface. Then the teacher seized the student's head from the rear and held him in the water for what seemed to the student ages. Finally, the teacher let the student up for air. The student burst from the water gasping. When the student had finally gotten his breath, the teacher asked, "While you were under the water, what did you want more than anything else?" The student exclaimed, "Air, I needed air; I could not breathe!" The teacher said, "You must want God just as much. Just as you could think of nothing more than having air in your life, so you must want God in your life with just as much determination." So must the Ascension Master desire Source. This does not mean that problems in life will disappear or that life will suddenly become effortless. What it does mean is that if your eye is constantly on Source, everything else will take on the proper proportion.

Do you remember the movie, "Oh, God"? John Denver, walking alongside George Burns, in Burn's role as God, asked Burns, "What will I do, I've lost MY job, I can't get a job in this city." Burns replied, "Lots of cities, lots of jobs." By no means is this meant to demean the challenging and sometimes terrible circumstances in which we find ourselves. The great master Paul Twitchell often wrote of being nearly broke and down to his last two quarters, yet he nearly always saw the way in which his circumstances provided him with yet another opportunity to resonate even more so with the Source energy and with the goal of achieving, in his context, God Realization.

Understand that no circumstance can present itself to you that, in some way, does not heighten your immersion in the Source. That's just the way it is. Your challenge is to recognize it and to align yourself even more so with the Source of all life. How this is done has been mentioned in so many ways in this discourse. This is by resonating with love at some level, in full consciousness of God's love. This will help the individual to gain a useful perspective when enmeshed with problems and to see the problems from a higher point, which is illustrated in the following spiritual exercise.

Note the particular problem on which you are focused. Look at the details. Notice your sense of self, in terms of how you feel, where you seem located, spiritually. If the problem feels overwhelming, do not be surprised. That is perfectly normal. Do not be surprised if you do not feel a sense of spiritual location. That is only normal.

Now, allow your attention to rest gently on whomever you look to for your ultimate healing and spiritual development. If you do not have one, then, for the purpose of this exercise alone, you may place your attention on the Ascension Master vortex (not the personality, Gregory, but the energy vortex that supports the Ascension Master work.) In order for the exercise to work, your attention needs to be on a person or being that can serve as a spiritual vortex, based on your experience or on the claims made on his or its behalf.

Now, put your attention on the problems simultaneously. Overlay the image of the spiritual person or Ascension Master vortex onto the problems. Allow yourself to experience the effect of the combination of the two. Now, examine the problems separately, keep the awareness of the spiritual object in the back of your mind, as it were. Let your attention gently wander, see what now occurs to you about the problem, in terms of its significance, possible solutions or other dimensions of the problem. Once you have an insight that seems harmonious, fill yourself with gratitude.

It is now important that you ground the energy. Take your journal out and write a complete description, step by step, of what you did. This will transfer to your unconscious and make even more automatic the use of this technique when you face other problematic situations. Eventually, you will stabilize in the Source energy and see all problems from the Source perspective, to the extent that there stop being problems and simply are situations and opportunities for spiritual service and growth opportunities, if you will, to give and receive even greater amounts of Source love.

In this lesson, a great amount of information has been shared, information that has been deliberately constructed to help open your heart and to align you more fully with Source, and, in so doing, the Source that is within you manifests in the Source that is you, and you become and are the light that illuminates and heals the world, greeting all whom you meet as the embodiment of Source.

Gregory

So, take a moment to inventory, calibrate and measure the strength of your faith, because that is where your journey and life in MY heart begins and ends, so to speak. Actually, of course, it does not end here. More correctly, this is where it transcends all that you know and think you know. Have faith!

Printed in the United States
By Bookmasters